MY FAMILY

MY FAMILY

A PORTRAIT IN LETTERS

My Family

Cover design by Maia Ballis.
Back cover photo by Tom Foster.

2nd Edition

Printed in the USA and UK on acid-free paper.
Published by:

 Robertson Publishing™
www.RobertsonPublishing.com

In collaboration with Vinegar Weed Press,
and support from Diane Morninglight

DEDICATION

To the grandchildren of Sidney and Loretta Raycraft, from the eldest, Kelli to the youngest, Gus. And to James, Joseph, Stephen, Miranda, Evan, Andrew, Elizabeth, Kyle, Hayley, Gwen, Sam, and Donovan in between.

This is your heritage, the memory of people who passed through your destiny, in Isabelle Allende's words. May you treasure and expand its legacy in your lives, now, and as you grow to assume responsibility for those who follow.

Reading these letters, I hope you feel about your grandparents' and parents' generations something of what the Russian novelist Leo Tolstoy said of his Aunt Toinette, who raised him.

> *Her chief influence upon me was, from childhood, to make me feel the spiritual joy of loving. I could see and sense how happy she was to love, and I understood this happiness.*

I have experienced the happiness that witnessing and sharing love creates. I believe the letters uniquely portray that happiness. I hold the vision that *My Family: A Portrait in Letters* deepens your capacity to feel the spiritual joy of loving, and pass it on.

"Aunt Sue" Susan Raycraft

ACKNOWLEDGMENTS

I am grateful to all the teachers and guides, friends and relatives who have helped me with this book.

My writing partner Diane Morninglight; editor Jenny D'Angelo; reader and cover designer Maia Ballis; photograph editor, Fred Kenyon; portrait photographers Tom Foster and Shae Lorigan; formatter, Paula Getzelman, and longest-lasting friends Kaede Lafferty and Joan Haukom, who knew me when the events portrayed transpired. Each provided invaluable help. I also thank Connie Bauer and Mark DeHart for their finish line rescues.

I acknowledge John Anderton for reminding me of the value of this work just before dying, and his spirit for guiding my final days of writing. John joins my birth father Sidney and father-in-love Bob Woodfill in the trio of wise, loving men I am blessed to call Dad. After Bob's death John married Jewell Woodfill, my husband Larry's mom.

Jewell taught me the value of time spent playing games, reminding me of the importance of the small affairs of daily living. I married into a family whose members are as devoted to each other as my own, for which I thank Larry.

I thank him too for being the kind of husband who expects and encourages me to follow my path without bending it to accommodate him. He and Dad would have been great friends.

CONTENTS

INTRODUCTION

I remember pouring hot water on my sleeping brothers when I was five. The incident created an impact which remains vivid nearly seventy years later.

We had moved into a two-story house in Concord, where I got a separate bedroom, one of the perks of being the only girl in the family. Sleeping with my brothers while my bed was being repaired, I remember taking the hot water bottle I was using down the stairs into the living room. After asking my father to loosen its lid, I refilled it at the bathroom sink. Then I crawled back into bed between Tom and Jim, unscrewed the lid I hadn't tightened, and dumped that hot water on both of them. I distinctly remember begging my shocked and screaming brothers, "Don't cry, it'll dry by morning."

Both parents responded, and when my father realized what I had done, he spanked me until my mother intervened to stop him. That's all I remember of that night.

Every few years afterward, at the dinner table or gathered around the TV, one of my siblings would bring it up. "Remember the time Susan poured the hot water bottle on us?" My father would glare at me, raise his hand in mock anger and say, "Every time I think of that I get so mad!" What angered him most was that I had planned my action and enlisted his help in carrying it out.

I am publishing this memoir sixty-eight years later. I never imagined the story of my five-year-old, mean-girl self would pop up. From the perspective of today, I believe that five-year-old self is here to make me honest, to push me to speak my truth.

A copy of the family performing on a neighbor's early home recording equipment from the year before the hot water bottle incident exists, of which I have no memory. Coached by my father, I say very emphatically, "I'm Susan, Susan Mary Raycraft, four years old!"

It feels to me that little girl also showed up to represent my early identity. She helped shape my character, growing up female in a patriarchal society, the only girl among six boys until age eleven. I learned to care for others and adapt my opinions and interests to please them. Not until leaving home in my twenties did I discover that I didn't much care for sports; I had learned to talk baseball that I might have a voice at the table.

Thanks to Mary Karr, whose book, *The Art of Memoir,* inspired me to reach back for the voice and spirit of that ornery little one as I make sense of the life she went on to live.

This book celebrates family, mine in particular. Writing it I have become keenly aware how dramatically a family shapes the characters of the children. My father's swift and dramatic discipline in the hot water bottle incident taught me to consider the reasons for my actions as well as their consequences. As that lesson got reinforced many times over the years, I learned within the safe boundaries of family to take responsibility for my behavior rather than project my feelings onto others whom I could blame for my choices.

My family also taught me how spiritual practice helps create unity and a sense of shared values. We prayed the family Rosary together, actually on our knees, for many years. We said Grace before every meal, adding our caveat, "May the Lord provide for the needs of others" to the standard version in the early sixties, probably at my suggestion.

Comparing my upbringing to others' over many years convinces me that my family experience is worth sharing. My parents prepared the family they created to deal with all the challenges of life, including shocking loss. Our response to the sudden deaths of father and brother Jim within five years of writing the letters, I believe demonstrates the effects of their parenting. We united as a family to care for one another. We focused on maintaining the quality of life that had always nourished us. And we held tight to our common heritage of love.

I received nineteen letters from my parents, Sidney and Loretta Raycraft, and the three youngest of their nine children—Philip, Cathy, and Mary—as I traveled in Europe on my "coming of age" journey at twenty-two. The letters capture a particular time in the life of the family. There would never be another summer like the one they record, when the family, which also included its eldest children—Tom, Jim, Gerry, Don and John—still lived together in its rambling two-story home in Los Angeles while I traveled in Europe.

The letters are like archeological treasures, providing an intimate view of the family's daily life. The rhythm was slow and steady, attuned to small changes and recurring patterns. Blending disparate personalities, ages, and experiences into a harmonious whole, for the purpose of developing each, it bound eleven individuals together in a well-functioning unit.

My family created a crucible which taught its members how to build relationships infused with respect. People are often astonished to hear that of the eight siblings in my family, not one is divorced from their original marriage partner. One of the reasons we all remain married is that we Raycrafts learned you don't quit relationships. You may ignore them and play with someone else for a while, but when you're ready, that person is still there, and you deal with them, whether or not you ever address the deeper causes of conflict. In our family, you usually didn't—one of the lessons from my upbringing which continues to challenge me.

We all live with family for the long haul. It is a part of each of us; it shapes us. Unlike so many people, I was fortunate to be formed by a family that functioned well. Over decades, many friends have told me that mine is one of very few such families they know. Relatively speaking, we were that wholesome family in the TV sitcoms.

A primary reason for writing this book is to acknowledge and honor the parents responsible for that family. I seek to distil from the letters and explore the essence of their influence on me. I understand how these principles and values, which I learned from them, have guided me in my life:

1. Valuing home and a deep connection to family and community.

2. Seeing the importance of spiritual life and practices.

3. Discerning a child's behavior as it subtly reflects an emerging personality and development of character and providing constructive feedback to the growing child.

4. Teaching a child to become self-observant so that they will come to understand what underlies their behavior.

5. Modeling a range of disciplinary tools.

6. Understanding the enormous impact of small actions repeated over time.

My parents consciously chose the family they would build; it didn't just happen. Mother shared how she and Dad spoke of their expectations and desires during their courtship. Both agreed they wanted a lot of children, whom they would send to Catholic schools. That educational choice was not available to them, and it became a shared commitment, one they carried out despite its financial burden.

These photos of Sidney Raycraft and Loretta Wujcik were likely taken in 1938, the year both graduated, Dad from the University of Minnesota, and Mom from Virginia Junior College

Neither parent shared many stories of their pasts with us kids. Loretta and Sidney Raycraft lived fully in the present. As Mom approached eighty, my brother Gerry and his wife Chris found her preparing to throw away a photo album and two scrapbooks from her early life. She said, "Oh, no one is interested in these old things." I am grateful they saved them, as half the pictures in this book come from that collection. She had never shared, nor even mentioned having them, and only occasionally referred to the time in her life they reflect.

In October 2016, I traveled with Gerry and Chris to Two Harbors, the northern Minnesota town where Dad was born and raised. It's about 90 miles from Mom's birthplace in Virginia, Minnesota, where they met in 1938 or '39. Cousin Terry Raycraft hosted us and drove us past the high school from which he graduated in 1950. He explained Dad had graduated from the same school, housed in an older building, in 1934.

Terry said the same teacher, C.P. Wagner, who was a fixture at the school from before World War I until 1946–48, taught them both. Dad took mechanical drafting from him at the old school, as did his three brothers, one of whom was Terry's father, our Uncle Blair. My brother, James Blair, was named after him.

When Terry took that same class fifteen years later, one of his classmates bragged that his drawings were perfect. "I'll show you perfect drawings," Mr. Wagner told the proud student, and Terry saw his Uncle Sidney's name on them.

As he explained in an email to me later: "C.P. had a storage drawer for mechanical drawings that dated back many years. He only kept the best of the best. I was as pleased as you are now to find that Sid's drawings were included among the chosen."

Like Mother with her scrapbook mementos and photos of her past, as far as I know Dad seldom if ever, told his children this or other stories of his early life. I believe my parents' attention to living each day fully, focusing on the commitment to the family they built together, helps explain their reticence to share stories of their early activities and accomplishments. Absolute attention to the family they co-created was their life work, their oeuvre d'art. It left little space for the past.

I am who I am because of Loretta and Sidney Raycraft's co-creative endeavor. Sharing this inheritance guides my life and inspires this book.

These letters carry me beyond my family to the realm of universal connections to home and community all beings share. In the twenty-first century, people frequently leave their countries and families of origin. They seek to hold on to experiences of homelands and traditions they've fled due to war, natural calamity, and political upheaval. They strive to maintain or re-create families imbued with values learned from their parents, extended families, and cultures in entirely new and unfamiliar surroundings.

I intend that this book, focusing on my unique yet universal experience, encourages others striving to create healthy families in such circumstances.

May these simple letters, with their attention to the small details of daily living, inspire those striving to preserve and pass on values that have united and inspired families in every culture, country, and continent throughout the ages.

Finally, it is my intention that my words and those of my parents gift my nieces, nephews, and the greats who follow the presence of the wise ancestors most of them never knew personally. I invited their parents — my siblings — to contribute memories as a way to further that intention. I hold the vision that knowing Sidney and Loretta Raycraft and their Aunt Su through this book enriches all their lives.

What we have heard and known,
Things our ancestors have told us,
We will not keep from our children.
We will tell the next generation
. . . even the children yet to be born.
~ Psalm 78

Like the one with arms interlinking on the cover,
this photo captures Mom and Dad's close connection.

It was taken June 6, 1942, after they were married in a
Delaware church following early morning Mass

Every instant disappears in a breath and immediately becomes the past: reality is ephemeral and changing, pure longing. With these photographs and these pages, I keep memories alive; they are my grasp on a truth that is fleeting, but truth nonetheless; they prove that these events happened and that these people passed through my destiny. . . . In the end the only thing we have in abundance is the memory we have woven.

~Isabelle Allende

Portrait in Sepia

CHAPTER ONE: ANCHORED TO HOME

Letter 1, from Mother: **"Just a Note *To Let You Know We're All Well.*"**

Postmarked June 18 and received at a friend's in North Bergen, New Jersey, on June 21, 1966. In all the letters, I've left spelling and punctuation as written. They appear in italics to set them apart from my comments.

Dear Sue,

I'll send this air mail — hope you get it before you leave for Europe.

Not that I have very much to write but just a note to let you know we're all well.

You got an invitation to Jonie's shower. I sent a set of mixing bowls with her mother. Was glad I could tell her about your trip. Jonie is getting married the last of July instead of Oct.

Dad is chaperoning a teen-age dance at St. John's. The graduating 8th grade was invited — so Jopo went. My, what one week can do to change a boy. From a little boy, Jopo became a teenager.

His graduation was very nice. Fri. the 10th they had an assembly & Jopo walked away with 7 awards. "Boy of the Year," Honors, Service, History, Math, Choir — oops, missed one. Then on Sat. he got a religion award — a brand new missal. Now it's all Peggy!

Phil starts summer school Mon. but he's been wheezing some to-day. Hope it won't develop into anything too much.

Well, we got your furniture in your room and it looks real nice. Dad still hasn't put the mirror up yet. I'm washing all your clothes — some I'll wear, others I'll just pack away. I bought a new bedspread for the girls' bed and it looks pretty good. Shifted the furniture around — got rid of those old school desks & one chest of drawers.

1

It was so nice all of us going out for dinner — I really had a good time. Dad was in rare form — don't you think? Say a prayer that things will work out for Dad. Wish he'd just get a regular job.

We did a tape Sun nite to send to Tom. It sounded real good. Dad talked for over ½ of it and then the rest of us filled in.

Went out to dinner with the Quinns last nite. Peter came to pick up his family. Margaret is so happy about going to N.Y. John Bartuska is coming for his family the 4th of July weekend. I guess we'll have them, the Ryans and maybe the O'Connells over for a BBQ that Sun. It's really quite sad about everyone leaving.

Well Sue — best of luck & have a good time.

Love, Mother

I determined early in the book's genesis that my comments on the letters would be important. I soon realized insights from my siblings could greatly enhance my reflections. I invited their comments, which appear throughout the book. Thank you to all who added to my understanding of what growing up Raycraft means, and for allowing me to share your experience.

I received the letters this book memorializes as I zigzagged across Western Europe during the summer of 1966 on my "coming of age" adventure.

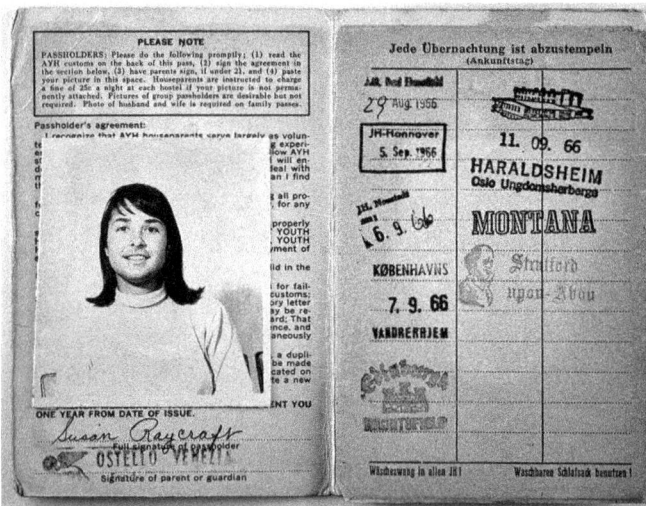

The passport that opened the door to a world of adventure I'd only imagined.

2

The letters chronicled my family's daily life, anchoring me to home as I traveled the world. I remember standing in line at various American Express offices to claim them, and then reading them over and over. The letters accomplished the purpose my mother sets here; they let me know my family was all right.

They catalog the small, repetitive activities of family life that molded my character and that of my eight siblings. My brothers Tom and Jim received similar letters during those years, as they came of age at Air Force pilot training during the Vietnam War.

I received this first one the day before boarding a London-bound plane at JFK Airport in NYC. Liberated from family by two years at Cal Berkeley, and now traveling abroad, I could feel my life and my sense of self change. The letter writers' lives were also changing significantly, as Mom implies in her last line above, "It's really quite sad about everyone leaving."

She refers to the families of men my father worked with at Shell Chemical Company's Synthetic Rubber Division in Torrance, California. He had been transferred there from Shell's San Francisco office in 1959, moving his large family into a lovely home in Leimert Park, an unincorporated section of Los Angeles. There Sidney and Loretta Raycraft and their nine children began a love affair with the Southern California lifestyle.

Seven years later in 1966, Dad's unit was disbanded and most of its staff transferred to Shell's New York City division. It was a sad time; the families had become close friends during those years of shared experiences.

Dad made a startling choice. Rather than accept the company's offer of a job in New York, he decided to live on vested retirement from his twenty years with Shell, and explore career options that allowed him to remain in Los Angeles. Exchanging the California life he loved for the stress of a daily commute to New York City appealed neither to him nor the rest of the family, particularly his wife.

My father's choice seemed to bring him more joy than apprehension. I was a senior at UC Berkeley as these changes unfolded, just before the possibility of a post-graduation trip to Europe surfaced. One of my most treasured memories is Dad telling me his momentous decision during one of his last visits to Shell's San Francisco office.

I heard his plan over a fish dinner in the corner of Spenger's Grotto, near the Berkeley Pier. I was stunned and deeply touched, and can still hear him saying these words to me:

"In the twenty years I've worked for Shell, I can only recall a few things I'm truly proud of. They all involved my telling young guys new to the company what I thought lay ahead for them, and one even decided to leave based on that information.

I want to do work I feel good about for the rest of my life, perhaps something with inner city hospitals, or bringing new technology into colleges. And maybe someday, I'll just be a wise old grandfather," he finished with a grin.

He told me that Mom had agreed to give him one year to explore his options before he decided how he would support the family, which stunned me almost as much as his decision. I would be graduating and getting a job; the two oldest boys had five-year Air Force commitments when they graduated from Loyola University; Tom was already in pilot training for Vietnam.

Dad was the sole support of another six children, ranging in age from ten to eighteen. How could he afford to set off on his own? How had he talked Mom into this plan? The only explanation I could imagine was that her aversion to moving to New York trumped her fear of the unknown.

I was impressed. I thought about how different my dad always seemed from other men of his generation. He was youthful, loved bow ties, and wore his hair in a perennial crew cut.

This man so many called "Dad" was unique in many ways. I was the only girl I knew among my high school acquaintances who attended performances of the Los Angeles Philharmonic with her father, climbing the stairs to the upper rows, cringing at his complaints about the poor seats I paid for myself.

During the warm LA summers, he often joined his work buddies to play beach volleyball. He kept in shape by jogging around the pool, years before jogging hit the national consciousness. I still treasure a worn copy of his workout bible, the "First U.S. Edition of the Official Royal Canadian Air Force Exercise Plans for Physical Fitness," published by This Week magazine in 1962.

It was spring 1966 when he took me to that Berkeley restaurant, just a few months before I would graduate from the University of California with a bachelor's degree in Sociology. I had transferred to Berkeley for the 1964 fall semester, after attending Mount St. Mary's College for two years while living at home. My timing was perfect. I witnessed the start of the Free Speech Movement and joined campus demonstrations and teach-ins against escalating the war in Vietnam.

Change swirled about me. The Civil Rights movement began to get the nation's attention. College students from across the country traveled to the South to register voters during the summer of '64. People I knew personally marched across the Selma Bridge in 1965. Proud of my membership in the generation of change symbolized by Berkeley in the sixties, during spring break I was invited to explain to a Los Angeles businessman's lunch group what the young generation was doing up there.

Unwilling to ask my Reagan-admiring father for scarce money to finance my college education at a left-learning, headlines-grabbing campus, I returned home each summer to work for Shell at clerical jobs available to offspring of mid-level managers. I envied friends who worked in Mexican villages with the Newman Center's Amigos Anonymous or traveled to the South to sit in for civil rights while I spent my summers working for Shell and living at home.

Now as I neared graduation, my conservative father was talking to me about how he too might change the world. He mentioned my connections with an inner-city parish when he shared his imagined future as a man free to make new choices.

He'd graduated from the University of Minnesota in 1938, married in 1942 and started his large family. After working in corporate sales for twenty years, he was forty-seven at the time of that conversation, an old man to me. Sitting across from him at the table that day, I felt we'd become comrades facing the unknown together.

I learned later that my older brother and Dad corresponded about starting a business together after Tom returned from Vietnam and finished his Air Force service. Though ahead of his time in many ways, Dad was not a budding feminist; neither of us envisioned business partnerships for father and daughter in those days. Besides, I wanted to serve people as a social worker, not make money off them.

5

The dinner Mom refers to toward the close of this first letter was probably in early June. They drove up from LA to get my things, freeing me to leave for my European adventure. We went to a favorite restaurant of theirs on the road between Berkeley and Concord, the town where the family had lived for a decade before moving to Berkeley in 1957.

My mother's asking me to say a prayer "that things will work out for Dad," while wishing "he'd just get a regular job," touched me deeply. While she had absolute faith in her husband of twenty-four years, she was a worrier. Her sister, our Aunt Marie, once described hearing Dad tell her, "If it helps you, go ahead and worry, but it does absolutely no good for any other reason."

This first letter presages those that followed in its chronicling of daily life in the Raycraft home. From graduation awards to school starting in the fall, from Dad chaperoning a school dance to Mom planning a Fourth of July gathering, everyone's life matters.

The letters focus on the activities of the younger kids who were home most. They had the time and inclination to write me letters of their own, usually appended to those of their parents. The four oldest were working and building lives outside the family orbit, entering college and the Air Force.

I kept all the family's letters, along with the letters and cards I wrote them from Europe, for the next half-century. I'd occasionally dig them out of storage boxes and drawers and read through them. Each time I reread the letters, I encountered my middle-aged parents, their simple words and loving attention to family.

Every reading allowed me to revisit the naïve, open, and incredibly vulnerable girl I was at twenty-two. I called men boys and was still very much a girl myself, or a "colleen" if my admirer happened to be Irish.

I always felt the story the letters held was worth sharing. I vaguely intended to write it and occasionally dabbled at doing so. I began serious work in 2004, as I turned sixty. Chapter 14, "Together Again", details the influences that finally led me to commit to the work, which would take another 13 years to complete. Those close to me have heard about it for years, and it is my hope that the reading is worth the wait.

Christmas card to the Raycraft family, drawn by school friend Linda Pardo, in 1958

CHAPTER TWO: ROOTS AND WINGS

Letter 2, from 11 Year-Old Cathy: *"I Wish I Was With You."*

I received three letters in a single envelope postmarked July 6, which I picked up in Madrid, Spain on July 14, 1966. As mentioned previously, I've left spelling and punctuation as written.

Dear Sue

How are you?

Dear Sue,

How do you like Europe? Pretty neat hah?

After two false starts, Cathy completed her letter:

Dear Sue, I got your letter today so I decided to write. The Ryans & Bartuskas are coming tomorrow. I like the furniture an aful lot. The first week the room was aful clean, but now its kind of a mess. But I'll try to keep it clean. One of my 12ve year molers are coming in. It really hurts. Mom took me to the dentist yesterday. We found out it was infected so he took out some of the gum so the tooth could come in but it still hurts. Every since school got out Mary & I been going to Mass we sing every morning. The singing is all right. Sometimes its better than other days. Today were going to the movies. We saw the "Sound of Music" It was so good I want to see it again. Today were going to see Born Free & The Trouble with angels. I got 8 A's on my report card. I wish I was with you. It would be so fun going to all those places. Mom made me a bathing suit (two piece) She also made me a dress she's making me a summer skirt (should be nice) What time do you get up. I get up at 7:00 every morning & on Sun. 6:30. pretty early heh! I swim most of the time. But I haven't been going in because of my tooth. Every hour I have to put warm water with one teaspoon of salt. It doesn't taste to good well someone going to continue this letter now. By, thanks for the card, Cathy

Letter 3, from Mother: ***"It must be wonderful seeing all the things you've heard about."***

Dear Sue,

Jerry got a card from Paris today – I thought it was from you & here its one of his "girl friends." They just love Paris. How did you like it?

It seems you're going thru these countries fast! Are you planning on going back to them on your way back?

Planning a party for Cathy tomorrow – a swimming party. Hope they have fun. I got Cathy a shoulder purse & a daily missal for her birthday. She wants to go up & visit Barbara Trapp – so if I can arrange with someone going up, I'll send her up for a week or so. I can send her up with John Ryan but I'm hoping one of Kathy Trapp's friends will take her up.

Had the Ryans, Bartuskas & Zee O'Connell here Sun. for a Barbeque. We had a real nice time. O'Connells haven't sold their house, so she's staying here until she does. The Bartuskas left yesterday. John Bartuska said that he could meet your plane when you came back. By the way which airline are you flying?

Cece Brewer & Wayne have been going around quite a bit. Don't quote me but Mrs. Brewer said they were quite serious.

I've been washing & cleaning your clothes & just packing them away. Have been sewing a little but can't say I'm accomplishing much.

We got a wedding announcement from Jonie Hummes. – you did too. They are getting married July 30th. Eliz Campbell was married – I saw her picture in the Tidings.

Dad & I are thinking of going to Tom's graduation or "wings" ceremony on Oct 26th. Dad's sister lives near San Antonio & it would make a nice visit. Lots of things may happen but we are hoping you'll be home by then and it will be easier at home then.

Are you enjoying your trip? It must be wonderful seeing all the things you've heard about.

Have a wonderful time – I'll try & write more next week – so that you'll get more than one letter. Love, Mother

Letter 4, from Dad: *"Regards To All My European Friends And Enjoy Yourself."*

Dear Sue & Fellow Travelers,

By now, I suppose you're debating whether you should ever come home. I'm kidding, of course, but I do hope you are encountering enough hospitality (and tolerance) to make the trip interesting <u>and</u> enjoyable.

Events at home are nice and quiet with no undue problems at the moment. We just bought a new car today, so perhaps that will introduce some new problems.

I tried calling Fr. George but he's out till late so I probably won't get to talk to him before mailing this. Anyhow, he's still here.

We are still exchanging tapes (recordings) with Tom, and all is well with him. Tomorrow, July 6 is "big" Cathy' birthday – hooray!

The 4th of July passed quietly – no rumbles in Watts although many were fearful.

Regards to all my European friends and enjoy yourself.

Love, Dad

From Cathy's, "Wish I was with you. It would be fun going to all those places," to both parents' heartfelt wishes that I have a good time, these three letters illustrate my family's support and encouragement of all its members. Dad's comment that he hoped we encountered "tolerance" captures his satirical edge.

The opportunity for my unexpected European adventure came up just before I was to graduate from Cal. A friend who had already booked the student charter flight leaving New York for London canceled at the last minute. Her travel companions urged me to join them in her place.

I couldn't imagine how that might be possible and called my parents to ask what they thought. I had no income, had to ask for a loan, and was unsure when I could repay them.

Without hesitating, and with his usual foresight, Dad encouraged me. He said there would never be a better time to see the world, and agreed to lend me the money. Perhaps his uncertain future inspired his urging me to seize this opportunity of a lifetime.

I'm the only traveler holding on to a pack as we three travelers pose with an American serviceman whose family adopted us in Copenhagen

Friends and college room-mates, Dale Wright, Cathy Downs and I left Berkeley "midst tears," at 10:30 AM on June 13, 1966, in a "Drive-Away" car we contracted to deliver to New York City.

I know the place, time and tearful nature of our departure thanks to the 3x5 pocket calendar I carried with me for the entire trip, documenting highlights of each day's adventures. I was already an historian at twenty-two.

I also carried a spiral notebook in which I recorded names and addresses of people we met, places to stay recommended by those people, and contacts we might look up along our route. A few lists of expenses capture the incredibly low cost of travel in 1966. They record meals ranging in price from $2.80 to $5.15, which we split three ways.

By staying in youth hostels and hitchhiking, three full months of travel cost in the neighborhood of $500, about how much our favorite travel guide, *Europe on $5 A Day,* projected.

After a couple of days sightseeing in London, we ferried across the English Channel. In Bruges (Brussels) we hitchhiked for the first time to the youth hostel at the edge of town. We soon left Belgium for a full week in Paris. Awed by museums and art galleries, I suffered sore feet and new shoes (still not of the walking-for-miles variety). We visited several castles in southern France then headed for Spain.

These three letters awaited me in Madrid. They describe activities back home, and my parents' daily involvement in their children's lives. They knew what all nine of us were doing, and followed our friends' activities as well; nothing seemed to escape their watchful interest.

Dad's addressing his letter to "Sue and fellow travelers," and closing with regards to his new European friends illustrates this quality of connection.

He also mentions trying to contact my friend Fr. George, the pastor of a nearby church who shared my commitment to ecumenical Catholicism and the struggle for civil rights. Fr. George was about to be transferred, and Dad hoped to meet with him before he left LA.

Dad may have wanted to discuss possibilities for his future. Fr. George was the pastor at St. Raphael's, the inner city parish Dad referred to when sharing thoughts about where he might focus his energies after leaving Shell. This is in a conversation described in the first chapter.

Finally, his mention of "rumbles in Watts" refers to the family home's proximity to where the preceding year's riots had taken place.

My parents also expected us to relate to their world. Mom's considering asking one of their friends to transport ten-year-old Cathy from Los Angeles to San Francisco illustrates the extended family network of which we were a part.

I knew their friends well enough to contact the recently transplanted "Shell Crowd" in New York City on my return trip. They arranged to meet me for lunch as their guest at an expensive restaurant. One of the men asked how much cash I had left after my travels. When I took out my wallet and found just $40, he said, "I wouldn't cross the street with that little money," and handed me a $100 bill.

Cathy's telling me that she loved the new movie, "Sound of Music" foreshadows events on another continent a couple of months later. After we met in Vienna, Fritz crossed Europe by motorbike to meet me in London, where we cried together at that same movie. Its melodies became "our songs" for the duration of the relationship.

In her letter, Mom suggests that my coming back home to live might allow her and Dad to take a vacation, and attend Tom's graduation from flight training. Helping my parents by taking over their responsibilities at home felt like a great way to repay their generosity in supporting my travels. I was in no hurry to be on my own and I felt honored to be trusted with care of the family.

CHAPTER THREE: A TRIBE OF NINE

Letter 5, from Mother: *"I'm So Glad You're Enjoying All The Wonderful Things Europe Has To Offer"*

Postmark illegible, dated July 10, received in Madrid, Spain on July 15, 1966

Dear Sue,

I'm going to try writing one more letter – hope you get it.

We're leaving in an hr or so to go to Balboa to see the Goodwins.

They have rented an apt for 2 weeks & have invited Cathy & Mary to spend the week. Isn't that great!

We've had a BBQ with the O'Reilleys – it was fun but it would have been better if I didn't have a sinus headache. It was nothing compared to the one I had 2 weeks ago but bad enuff so I couldn't enjoy myself. Jim O'Reilly had quite a bit to drink & he was funnier than heck.

Fri nite we went to the Music Center & saw "Funny Girl." We took the Clarks---they had never been there. We were standing there admiring the place & Rita Speltz came up & talked to us. She knew you were in Europe – she was at Doree's wedding. She's going to teach in Minn – Mpls or St Paul. She looked great.

Isn't that something – you had to go all the way to Europe to find out about Linda. One never knows – does one? That reminds me John Ranahan called last nite & talked to Dad. He flew down to some boy's house & they were driving down to Tijuana for the bullfight today & then flying back tonite. He took Father George's phone no. So I don't know if he got him. Dad's been trying to get in touch with Father George to take him to the track but hasn't been able to reach him.

Don has gone to the track with Cravens & yesterday he won $30 – Dad lost about that much.

Your letter was surely interesting. I'm so glad you're enjoying all the wonderful things Europe has to offer. I heard something on TV last week that just made me sick. Imagine Americans visiting in a foreign country protesting their government & their country. They're the only ones in the world that can raise their voices against their country & not be put in jail or shot — but to go out of their country & do this was sickening. I imagine they (the Communists) were especially happy when they burned the Am. Flag. Imagine burning our flag — they shouldn't be allowed back in this country, just send them on to Russia.

Haven't heard from Tom for quite awhile. In his last tape he mentioned that Ben Aranda's brother-in-law is an instructor there & he spoke up for Tom to go on his cross country to Los Alamitos Air base — so we may get to see him in Aug. Isn't that great!

Dad is still a man of leisure — Hasn't started fixing my living room yet but when he does — I'll surely dread that.

Guess this will be all until the next stop off place that you give us----
Love, Mother

In this letter, my mother told me I shouldn't be allowed back in the country, "Just send them on to Russia!" We had witnessed the Paris protests against US policy in Vietnam from the sidelines on that Fourth of July, and didn't participate in burning the American flag. While we agreed with the French protesters, armed police beating young people with clubs shocked us. And watching the news back home, my mother certainly didn't envision her daughter there on the street.

I was probably the source of more of my mother's frequent headaches (like the two described in this letter) than any of her nine kids. I am grateful she couldn't see me at that Paris street demonstration. That would have given her a big one.

In a similar vein, I recall Dad telling me sometime during my college years that he worried more about me than his other eight children combined. When I pushed for a reason, he said I was too sensitive or possibly too trusting, and he feared I'd be hurt.

While being the kid who caused her parents the most grief wasn't my intention, I admit I often held opinions and engaged in activities that differed from the rest of the family. I was the one who insisted on Bible studies and home Masses in the sixties, which the rest of the family participated in half-heartedly. That they were willing to take part at all is witness to the family sense of togetherness.

That community even reached me in Europe, as Mother marvels at in her letter. Learning of marriages, births, deaths and other news through the network of close connections, people we'd "run into" who knew others we knew—that happened all the time.

After Jim got bitten by a caged deer in Yosemite, our family stopped taking vacations, but we kids were often invited to accompany friends on theirs. Cathy and Mary's week on Balboa Island that Mom mentions here, and Don's camping trip, from which both parents describe his coming home filthy in other letters, are examples of that kind of exchange.

I've always believed our family's unique contribution to the extended family support system was providing a home everyone loved to visit. It felt like being at summer camp to spend time at the Raycrafts. There were so many of us running around that visitors became an extension of the family energy. Those from smaller families especially loved this.

I attended a birthday party for Dale's ninety-year-old mother when I began this project. Her brother Wayne described the downstairs of our large house "so full of kids it was like an auditorium." Wayne's love life is a frequent topic in these letters, as he married a good friend of all three of us.

Friends who visited our home experienced Dad's unique sense of humor. When I ran for student body president in my junior year in high school, my campaign manager spent two nights at the house working on election plans. As we gathered for our usual 6 PM dinner, she watched Dad sharpen a carving knife at the head of the table, with his flare for drama, and hesitated to sit near him.

On the second night of her stay, he introduced Jonie to another visitor as "a friend of Sue who's spending a week with us." When she protested that it had been only two nights, he added, "It just seems like a week."

For Mom's seventieth birthday in 1987, my brother Gerry and I video-transferred the repetitive 8 mm films taken of family life in the late fifties and early sixties. The younger kids opening Christmas presents, hunting Easter eggs, and jumping in the pool as they grew older and larger, plus a few graduations of the older ones, was their total content.

I selected as background music a song whose lyrics matched the repetitiveness of the scenes and captured the essence of the family life in which we grew up:

> *Welcome to the family; we're glad that you could come,*
>
> *To share your life with us, as we grow in love.*
>
> *And may we always be to you what God would have us be,*
>
> *A family, always there, to be strong and to belong.*
>
> *May we learn to love each other more with each new day.*
>
> *May words of love be on our lips in everything we say.*
>
> *May the spirit melt our hearts, and teach us how to pray,*
>
> *That we may be a true family.*

The spirit had melted our hearts and toughened our knees during the almost daily family Rosaries we gathered to pray in homes in three different California cities—Concord, Berkeley and finally, Los Angeles.

Believing the adage, "The family that prays together, stays together," my parents would lead us to the front of the local Catholic church each Sunday, where we occupied two pews. Sharing the traditions and rituals of Catholicism united us as a family. Such early experiences planted seeds for the spiritual path I have re-created in many forms and places throughout my life.

Growing up, I frequently joined Dad to attend daily Mass, which had been his spiritual practice for as long as I could remember. For my twelfth birthday, he gave me the same daily missal he used, which I treasure as part of the spiritual heritage he gifted me. The last hours I spent with my father, we prayed together at Mass.

In the early sixties, Mary, our youngest, staged family renditions of the popular TV game show, "The Newlyweds," pairing each of us with a sibling or parent. One of the questions she asked was, "If your partner sat next to you at Midnight Mass and you fell asleep, what would they do?" Everyone had an answer from having observed each other over the years.

At the time of these letters, those still at home attended Sunday Mass together. Though the family Rosary had become history, the bond enhanced by regular family prayer remains solid to this day.

Growing up as a member of a tribe of nine teaches you to value community, which Webster defines as "participation in common." While we had few local relatives, the family's deep involvement with each other, as well as local church, school, neighborhood, and work communities created an extended family.

Mom served as president of two different Mother's Clubs in various schools and cities. At Christmas, she baked dozens of batches of cookies and candies to share with the nuns who taught us.

Dad often assisted the priest at daily Mass and was active in Knights of Columbus and other church groups. He played beach volleyball with his work buddies, and both parents attended the limited sports events available for their kids to compete in at the time.

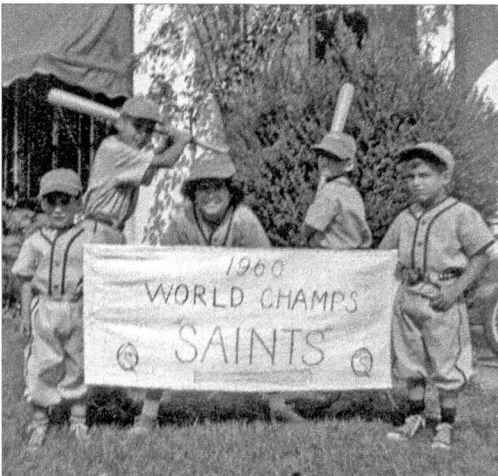

1960 WORLD CHAMPS: Mom sewed these uniforms for a school parade c. 1955. We played baseball on the vacant lot across the street, brown eyes against blue, with Dad pitching for both sides.

Their nine children's ages spanned just thirteen years. The family ritual that I loved most was welcoming each new addition. When Mom came home from the hospital with a new baby, we'd line up on the couch, in order by age, as she placed the infant into the arms of each successively smaller sibling.

I still remember the thrill of welcoming the new baby, who would become my special responsibility as the oldest girl, as well as a frequent replacement for the dolls with which other girls my age played.

I must have been about six when Dad discovered me dressing Don, my year-old brother, in clothes intended for a large girl doll. He was upset beyond my ability to comprehend, saying I was going to ruin that child.

Mom mentions dreading the living room renovation for the first time in this letter. Toward the close of the summer, Dad began gauging out the cracks which had emerged in the plaster and filling them with sheet rock mud in preparation for repainting. The resulting jagged lines occasioned an observation by then thirteen-year-old Philip, which has survived the ages, "Ho, ho, ho, it looks like roads!"

In his book, *Secrets of the Talking Jaguar,* Martin Prechtel explains that in the Mayan tradition, a person who needs healing asks the shaman to *"chumij"* or replaster him. Prechtel explains that repairing rickety houses ensures the smiley togetherness so missing in the preplanned, alienated lives of modern civilization.

CHAPTER FOUR: MOM'S IN CHARGE

Letter 6, from Mother: *"I'm Keeping All The Cards & Letters . . . How's Your Money Holding Out?"*

Dated July 19 and received in Barcelona, Spain, July 24

Dear Sue,

Received your letter today & was so glad to get it. Mrs. Young called me last nite to see if I had heard from you – it has been some time.

Cathy & Mary spent a week at Balboa Island with the Goodwins – coming home Sat. evening. Cathy took off Sun. for Daly City to visit the Trapps. Rose Bartolome went up to visit Kathy & it seemed like such a good idea to send her with one of the girls instead of Mr. Ryan. I went ahead & made the reservations for Cathy – poor Cathy it was so sudden.

Minnie came & spent Fri nite with me. Cathy came with her for a rest from the children. We went to Farmers Market Sat & then Sun Bob came with the children. Dad barbequed a turkey & we had a nice time.

Dad is following the stock & commodities market – goes there every morning after 6 o'clock mass. In the afternoon he works on the yard – today he went to the Races.

Got a tape from Tom & he called last week when he had soloed in the T38. He wasn't as excited as he was in the T37. He felt he could have done better but he did pass. He really likes flying. He said when he is low & depressed he can go up & its "Instant Motivation." I guess he's really found his niche.

I must wrap your present & mail it to Jonie. I ordered 3 sherbet glasses for her at $4 each, in Bullocks Wilshire no less. I was interested in China but I had to buy a whole place setting & that was $24 – thought it was too much. Dad doesn't want to go to the reception – I would like to tho. Jim leaves for summer camp the same day.

I'm chewing on Jucyfruit. I called Mrs. Brewer about going to see Msgr. This afternoon & Wayne answered the hone.

John has a sore throat & cold – took him to the Dr. & Phil in for his allergy shot. Mary had Marcie over for the nite & they are swimming now. Don has been working fulltime but only for a week – surely wish it could have been for a longer time.

Jim is going to have a frat. Rush party the Fri before he leaves for camp – just like Tom did – but Jim is a little more organized. Tom went shopping for his stuff the morning he left & I've already got Jim's marked & ready to go.

Your letter is so interesting! I've re-read it 3 times already. I'm keeping all the cards & letters – you'll probably want to see them all but you'll have all those wonderful memories that no one will be able to take away from you.

Your best bet will be to stick with Nick – Mr. Bartuska may be out of town or busy. The Quinnns & Toes' (Dad's boss) both bought houses back there & a week before they were to move in – the warehouse that was storing their furniture & personal belongings burned to the ground. Isn't that awful. Jopo, Mary & I are going to Bullock's Aug. sale this Fri – I'm taking them out to lunch. I wonder what kind of shoppers they are. I'm going to get some bras for myself – thought of getting some for you but better wait until you get home – seeing you're putting on weight!

How's your money holding out? I guess we could wire you some if we knew where to do it – so be sure & let us know.

Are you taking in the Bull Fights in Spain? How about Ireland? I thought you'd hit that before you went to France. Father O'Reilley will be back soon, so you'll miss him.

The social editor from the Mesa News called & wanted to know what our family was doing this summer. I said nothing. Then I remembered you were in Europe! It hasn't been in the paper as yet but I'll save it for you to see. She wanted your picture but I told her at another time. I told her about Tom & Jim going to camp & Cathy & Mary being at Balboa for a week – so I had something to tell her.

I think I've written just about all the news here. It surely isn't as exciting as your letters.

21

I'm glad you're remembering us in your prayers & you really have been hitting the cathedrals. Have fun, be good and all that jazz.

Love, Mother & all the rest

I'm mailing this out without getting anyone else to write – otherwise you won't get it in Barcelona.

This long, meandering letter is *so* Mom. Attentive to my schedule in the midst of her demanding life, she closes with an "executive decision" to mail it in time to match my schedule. She tracks each child's activities, including if I have enough money for my travels on another continent. Signing her letter "Love, Mother and all the rest" captures how closely she identified with her family.

Only three months into the full year her husband planned to explore new ways to support her and her children, she appears stoic. She lists his activities almost as though he were another of her kids, without seeming concerned about whether going to the races or working in the yard was moving him along a career path.

Her obvious delight that we were "hitting the cathedrals" inspired me to list each one we visited in my letters home.

Mother relished having something interesting to tell the social editor of our local newspaper, after first thinking she had nothing to brag about. Entitled, "Families Continue Flow of Activities," she kept the article published on July 21, 1966. I was thrilled to find it with the letters decades later, and include it on the following page.

She loved shopping at "Bullocks Wilshire, no less," which she once described to my friend Joan and me as "a cut above" other stores. While her life allowed limited time for impressing others, we kids knew appearances counted, and we felt her steady pressure on us to meet high standards.

She shares her decision not to send Cathy traveling across the state alone with one of Dad's friends. From time's perspective, I realize she's avoiding a situation that might have created impropriety or possible danger for her daughter.

In these letters from the middle years of her long career in motherhood, Loretta Raycraft's observations about her children are astute. She compares their styles and habits, like how differently her two eldest sons shop for the same fraternity party several years apart.

She assesses her daily choices and responsibilities toward each child in a clear, matter-of-fact manner. Asking about my needing money, shopping carefully for a gift for the girlfriend whose wedding I would miss, and suggesting I not depend on a family friend to meet us when we return all demonstrate her attentiveness.

And then she pauses to mention the kind of gum she is chewing. Joan told me she remembers how loudly Mom clicked her gum when she caught me doing the same. The ability to focus her considerable attention on what lay directly in front of her, no matter how large or small its significance, was my mother's genius. Today it's called "Living in the present moment," and is greatly admired.

Loretta's children often share memories of visiting her in the beloved Redondo Beach home she proudly bought on her own in 1972. There she lived alone for the last twenty-five years of her life.

The sea breeze blew through its louvered living room windows on a hot summer afternoon, and she'd exclaim as she opened the drapes, "Just feel that breeze, aren't we fortunate!"

Other funny Loretta-isms we laugh about are her Mother's Day tirades. She loved that all her children were a steady presence in her life. Those living nearby visited often, and the rest made regular trips to spend time with her.

Tuesday, July 21, 1966

Socially Speaking

Families Continue Flow of Activities

By BEBE LYONS

Scanning the activities of local families, the "energy-meter" is on a steady incline, for fathers are beginning to get the long awaited two week vacations and the truly warm weather is here. One of the most active families is the Sidney Raycrafts, 3454 West 48th Street. The family of nine children is currently speding the summer spread almost around the world. The most adventuresome is Susan, 22, who is touring Europe with a couple of school friends.

According to the last letter, they are enjoying the warm, friendly, yet spicy, country of Spain.

Miss Raycraft, who is a sociology graduate of the University of California at Berkeley, left in early June to tour the United States before departing for foreign shores.

Lieut. Thomas Raycraft, 23, is undergoing eight months of pilot training at Laughlin Air Force Base, Tex. He will graduate in October. Latest report shows he is flying T-38s.

A second son, James, 21, is also in the Air Force, but he is stationed in Houston at the basic training camp.

For most teen-agers, a summer just is not a summer without a trip to Balboa and Mary and Kathy Raycraft are making the most of it at the tiny island this week. It is probably the only place in California where you can ride a real auto ferry for just a few cents.

The rest of the children, according to Mrs. Raycraft, who just completed a term as president of St. John the Evangelist Mothers' Club, are at home.

Her wrath at the children of friends not as attentive to their mothers was a thing to behold. Here's how she puts it in a letter she wrote me in early April 1996.

"Mother's Day is for the birds! If kids can't see or talk to their mothers all year, forget Mother's Day. It's a big day for florists and card companies. It doesn't bother me if I'm home alone! Hope I'm not too negative?"

I often kidded her about that critical aspect of her personality to which she refers.

The Christmas season was always special in the Raycraft home, with Mom baking cookies and candy not just for us, but as gifts to the nuns who taught us and others. After leaving and starting our own families, we'd gather at her Redondo Beach home each Christmas Eve, sharing a tradition going back to our earliest days as a growing family — exchanging gifts with the one whose name you had picked.

Opening those gifts took hours, as the exchange grew to include all the spouses and children the nine of us had accumulated and produced.

She would shop all year for little things to stuff in the Christmas stockings she'd sewed for us as kids, which she scattered about the room before we arrived on Christmas Eve. She also delighted in making or buying the same thing to give each of us, from coffee grinders to ice cream makers, to homemade bath towel wraparounds with our names sewn on.

My favorite gift was a recipe book of our favorite dishes from childhood. She had previously given us spiral binders with copies of those typed recipes, made with a friend's help. This time she handwrote those same recipes with her arthritic fingers, in her still beautiful script, on pages of books she'd ordered printed with "The Raycraft's Family Recipe Cookbook" on the cover. The title page states:

> "With fondness these pages are completed and passed to others as a personal gift or a treasured family heirloom."

I wonder how many other mothers fondly wrote their recipes out nine times by hand.

I use this precious gift from my mother often. Each time, I delight in Mom's little comments about their sources, e.g., "I think Jerry got this recipe when he was in Taiwan from an Air Force Capt." (Mystery Pie), and "This is Phil's favorite—at least he always asked for it for his birthday," (Frozen Waldorf Salad).

About Pea Soup she wrote, "This is supposed to be the French Version of pea soup", and lists its source as "Sid's mother."

For one of the last Christmases we shared, I bought her Andrew Harvey's book, *Mary's Vineyard*. Its pages were filled with prayers and photos of the Divine Mother throughout the world. As I waited in line at a Santa Cruz bookstore for the authors' autographs, I over-heard the person ahead of me say something about how much more interesting it would be to travel the world taking photographs and writing than staying home to bake cookies.

I mentioned that my mother was the one who preferred to stay home baking cookies. Andrew assured me baking cookies was simply an-other way to manifest love, and inscribed the book, "For Loretta, In Mother Love, Andrew Harvey."

I added, "To my human mother, who so mirrors the Divine in my life, Your Daughter, Susan, Christmas 1996."

CHAPTER FIVE: FAMILY LIFE, SHATTERED

Letter 7, from 9 ½ year-old Mary: *"Each Day We Race Rocks As Horses"*

Postmarked August 1 and received in Rome, Italy, on August 6, 1966

Dear Sue,

Yesterday we went to Centenella and played tennis. Cathy and dad played a set dad won by three, dad had five and Cathy had two. It was really close. Cathy and I are taking tennis lessons again. Our new teachers are Joe and Mr. Bloodstead. there both pretty nice. I went to Bullocks for the first time with mom and Jopo. It was pretty exciting going to a big store. Mom bought me a skirt. Moms going to buy us some embroardery to start us off with a needle. Jim had a fraternity party Friday. We didn't want to stay home and listen to the noise, so we went to see a movie. We saw Help! and Around the World and Under the Sea. We had a paper drive if you get papers up to your head you could see the movie that they showed. Cathy and I went to Balboa with the Goodwins. We went to the beach everyday we were there. We went to Schark Iseland there we made a voodoo god out of clay. I brought a dollar and fifty cents and I had seventy cents left. We went bike riding, and sailing. Each day we race rocks as horses me horses are Admirably, Squad Leader, Tango, O'hara, The Hare, Real Good Deal, Maintain, Ter-Chi-Berzo, Turn True Blue, and Suislaw. Love Mary

Letter 8, from Mother: *"I'd Rather You Be a Mother Than A Tennis Player"*

Dear Sue,

I'll finish up this letter of Mary's & maybe Phils. Cathy mailed hers already. I went with them to play tennis but I didn't do too well. Phil said, "I'd rather you be a mother than a tennis player." Cute, ha? Dad

& I went to Jonie's wedding. Fr. Kelp from Loyola married them at St. Jerome's. It was a lovely wedding. The Hummes girls all looked alike, pixies, but real cute. Jonie was darling. We picked up Jim & went to the reception. I got Dad to go by saying Mrs. Hummes's mother would be there. She always made a big fuss about Dad. It was at the Sheraton Marina Hotel. It was a "sit down" affair but we didn't stay – it looked so crowded & it didn't seem like there was enough room, so we had a couple glasses of champagne & left. We met Ann Martin who had dated Tom – she wanted to be remembered to him. She said one of her brothers knew you from YCS. I didn't see anyone I knew from SMA except Julie Peycke. She's expecting & looked darling.

Read in the Mesa News that Sally Evans was married in June to some boy from Mt. Carmel – they were married at St. John Inglewood.

Talking about Mt. Carmel, Fr. George is being transferred to Our Lady of Mt. Carmel Church in Houston, Texas.

Jim left for summer camp Sat. afternoon. He didn't want us to go to the airport with him so Joe took him. The Frat party wasn't too bad, no one threw anyone into the pool & none of the neighbors complained. It wasn't too successful as far as rushees were concerned but lots of actives & alumni. Mike Conter (remember him, Jim's friend from Loyola High) was here & his date made a big fuss over Jerry. Mike asked Jerry what he was doing here & Jerry said, "I live here." Jerry & a friend had taken 2 girls out for dinner & came back here after. They were all dressed up in suits & looked pretty good. Haven't heard from Tom for awhile. Don went up to the mountains with the Ferdinands (from St. John's) for 4 days. Had a good time – came home dirty.

Mother

I received five letters in Rome on August 6, one from each of my faithful correspondents. Each letter celebrates the dynamic of family life in the Los Angeles home where the Raycrafts lived for fourteen years.

In their letters, all the young scribes mention a new game they'd invented. They'd roll small rocks named after famous racehorses down the sides of the swimming pool to see whose was fastest. Mary listed ten of her rocks' names, winning the prize for detail in letter writing. Cathy mentions just one, and Phil explains the rule that the rock going farthest is the winner.

Dad plays with four of his kids in Berkeley, just before moving to LA. From left, Jopo, Don (as Elvis) Mary, Dad and Cathy

The letters also reflect my parents' love of the casual lifestyle they enjoyed. They thrived in Southern California's weather, and its balance of anonymity with strangers and close ties to a chosen circle of friends suited them perfectly.

Both were born and raised in small towns in Northern Minnesota, Dad in Two Harbors, and Mom in Virginia. I am the only one of their children born in Minnesota. Moving to Northern California after Jim's birth in 1945, they raised their growing family in Concord until moving to Berkeley in 1957.

We heard occasionally that neither parent missed the Minnesota cold. Dad also shared he did not like growing up in a small town where everyone knew your business and discussed it behind your back.

The family arrived in Southern California at the start of the summer of 1959. In a pair of packed cars, we left the Berkeley home where we'd lived just two years, and drove south along the coast. After two nights at fancy hotels in Carmel and Santa Barbara, we lived for a couple of weeks in Long Beach, eating out at an upscale restaurant while waiting for a new home to become ours.

In the family's last vacation Jim was bitten by a deer in Yosemite, Mom discovered she was pregnant with Gerry, and Dad swore he'd wait until all his kids grew up before taking another one.

A dozen years later, we vacationed at Shell's expense because the company was transferring Dad to their Torrance synthetic rubber division. Enjoying this break from responsibility, Mom prepared to assume management of an even larger house than the one we'd left near Indian Rock in Berkeley.

I remember suffering from a rash during those two weeks, just like one I experienced when we moved from Concord to Berkeley. That was two years earlier, at the start of eighth grade; now I was leaving a new high school after my freshman year. Both moves came at crucial junctures in my life and challenged the good girl I always tried to be.

When we arrived at our new home on 48th Street, we were all thrilled by the luxury of this huge house just one block from Crenshaw Blvd, and a mile from the Catholic Girls' High School my parents had determined I would attend. I spent the first six months there trying to make everyone around me as miserable as I felt. I even caused my long-suffering mother to break down in tears after the ordeal of shopping for my new school uniform.

In 1961 I was elected St. Mary's Academy Student Body President. When I first met with the faculty advisor, Sister Carmelita, she recalled my attitude when she'd conducted my pre-enrollment interview and said she wouldn't even have admitted me had it not been for my father.

The family tolerated my negativity about the move and I finally got over it. We settled into our new surroundings, a two-story Spanish-style house and pool sprawled across two city lots. A spiral staircase provided entry from the swimming pool side, while a heavily landscaped, walled-in area led to a massive wooden door at the front. Gerry remembers the front entryway as a jungle with "plants in there (ferns? elephant ears?) that actually scared me." A third entry led to the laundry room and kitchen at the rear.

Family life revolved around the swimming pool. Flanked on one side by a full bath and storage room, and on another by a lanai complete with barbecue pit and telephone, grass sloped around the other two sides. Dad began grilling his favorite, marinated flank steak. Mom occasionally relaxed by sitting on the lawn pulling Bermuda grass, and all the kids took to the water.

John (whom we called Jopo) explained how the rock game described in letters to me was played.

And then there were the rock races in the pool!! GO, Native Dancer!! If you found the perfect "rolling rock" you hoarded it and would never put it back in the trough around the pool. The best part was having to dive down to the pool drain several times to determine the winner in a close race. That was probably the best lung exercise for Phil with his asthma but he seemed to 'win' lots of those 'photo finishes'. I don't think we thought much of the fact that we were creating currents of our own down there at the bottom of the pool which probably had to impact the finish.

Others pool games included jumping from the upper brick wall into the deep end and counting underwater laps to see who could swim most; I think Jim was the champion. Home movies from that time document pool play and lawn baseball games.

The swimming pool covered a city lot and brought the family together throughout the year. Mom recalls once swimming on Christmas Day!

The older boys were responsible for maintaining the pool and surrounding yard under Dad's watchful eye. John shares the deeper impact of those tasks, which affected us all:

A couple of things I learned from living at 48th Street. Dad assigned us weekend chores, and mine was to make sure there weren't any bird droppings on any of the walks around the yard and the pool. A bucket of water and an old broom or small brush were my tools of the trade. At the time I didn't much care for the task, but I now realize that in doing those chores I learned the valuable lesson that we all had to pitch in to keep that yard and house clean and livable.

Mary describes how the whole yard became Disneyland! "Every area of lawn was a different land, and we would "fly" in one area. I don't remember what we did in the others."

John recalls the approach to free time the family shared throughout our growing-up years:

Ah, necessity is the mother of invention!! I do believe that is how the "alphabet" game came into being. Someone was bored, and we wrote sentences from any magazine down the page in a column and then repeated a second column. Then, thought up famous people to match the initials. Of course, we added our own "Raycraft" twist to the game by allowing a good "bluff" name to pass as real.

The house on 48th Street had two large bathrooms and one half-bath. While working on this book, I learned for the first time that the four youngest kids used to "celebrate" Mass in the upstairs bathroom. Dual sinks in front of a huge mirror made the perfect altar.

Necco wafers became the Communion host, and the mirror made it quite theatrical, Mary and Cathy recall. While only the boys could be priests, the girls were "altar girls," several years before the Catholic Church allowed girls to serve at Mass. That upstairs bathroom was most unusual. The purple, black and yellow tile, black fixtures, raised tub and walk-in shower with dual shower heads created luxury and oddity we all loved.

Besides the lanai phone by the pool, five different colored phones throughout the house thrilled the family's teens. The sophisticated vacuum system housed in the basement, accessed by attaching a hose to outlets in each room, delighted Mom. And a built-in dishwasher, enhanced by the portable we brought, made us a two dishwasher family in an era when most families had none.

Mary recalls, "ONCE actually doing all the dishes by hand because I wanted to see what it would be like without the dishwashers."

Upstairs was the large bedroom that would become the "boys' dormitory," with a small one right off it whose occupant rotated as the brothers grew and left home. From its window an enterprising teen-age boy could escape via a drain pipe to go "joy riding" with a friend. Gerry has confirmed the rumor that Dad once had to fetch him at the local police station when he was caught doing that!

31

Also upstairs, across from the bath, was the master bedroom where Mary remembers Dad's talks to kids seated on the "long, white loveseat at the end of their bed." Cathy and Mary shared the small adjoining room, called the "sun room" for its wraparound windows overlooking the pool. A small room downstairs, dubbed "the out-the-back-door bedroom" was the prized possession of the oldest boy; it provided the best access to the freedom to come and go.

The family's new LA lifestyle was soon complete with a communal red Pontiac. Tom remembers being in a five-car pile-up coming home from Loyola University, after which that car "was never the same." He marveled when Dad asked only if his son was hurt when called at work with the news.

That small back bedroom, like the pool, looms large in individual memories. John recalls spending hours listening to the massive AM/FM radio Dad bought and the family shared, recording music onto a reel-to-reel tape recorder, on which we also recorded tapes to send Tom in Vietnam. He thinks it was a Zenith, but Phil remembers an Emerson.

When John left for college in 1970, Mom let him take the twin bed he'd slept on in that room, bought when Jim resided there. "I kept that bed for many years after; it was a Simmons mattress and oh so very comfortable," he remembers.

As I worked on creating this book, it became clear that the experience of my siblings could add a valuable dimension to our family's story. I reached out to them on several occasions, inviting them to share memories they would like to pass on.

Another car story unearthed in sibling recall of the house on 48th Street came from Gerry. Dad must have always wanted to rebuild a car, and enlisted Gerry's help in getting a 1960 white Ford Fairlane into the space between the two garages on the property.

Five decades later, Gerry proudly recalls Dad's praise for his driving that car up the steep, narrow driveway without hitting the lower garage wall or the retaining wall on its opposite side. He describes driving down Victoria Avenue "picking up enough steam, then turning at a high rate of speed into the driveway so that it would coast to the top without the engine doing any of the work."

Dad worked on that car during his last year, and I like to think he enjoyed the challenge, though it never ran again and had to be towed away after his death.

Between kitchen and living room was the red-tiled dining room, whose steps led down to the huge, green-carpeted living room. Over many years it provided space for a variety of family activities, such as ping-pong baseball games with carefully crafted rules: a single was past the pitcher, a double at a certain level on the bookshelves, a triple had to hit the curtains, and a home run was anything above the curtains. A rolled up *Life* magazine was the bat.

We'd open Christmas gifts, pray the family Rosary and celebrate an occasional home Mass in that sacred space. On rare and important occasions a family meeting would be convened. Large wooden beams and a massive mirror created a dramatic effect, and the older kids remember the thrill of descending its spiral staircase in prom dresses and tuxes, smiling for the camera. You can see the bottom of that staircase in the snapshot of the whole family on the cover and in Chapter Six.

My bedroom was on one side of the kitchen, while on its other side the TV room overlooked the swimming pool and lanai. We installed our small black-and-white TV, and it wasn't until perhaps the summer of 1965 that we got a color TV, which my parents actually bought with S&H stamps glued into hundreds of books.

It was in the TV room you learned to call "Saves," or you'd lose your place on the naugahyde couch. It was there I discovered in my early twenties that my father and brothers all had small feet. I still recall Dad's amazement that I had never noticed that detail before.

And it was in this room on May 2, 1967, I learned we lost our father.

That day began like any ordinary day. As was our occasional custom, I rode to 6 AM Mass with Dad in the blue MG Tom had left in his care while serving in Vietnam. I left for work and Dad went to the nearby office where he was the sixties version of a day trader.

I would never see him alive again. That day my father was stabbed to death in a neighbor's yard.

The neighbor across the street witnessed what happened. She testified at the subsequent murder trial that as Dad emerged from Tom's

MG, a car stopped on Victoria Ave. A man got out and followed Dad to a lawn across the street and began stabbing him with a huge knife.

Our neighbor yelled at the assailant to stop; he seemed not to hear. She watched, screaming, as he stabbed many times, then walked casually back to the car where his accomplices drove him away. She immediately called the authorities. By the time they arrived, Dad was dead. The knife was found the next day in a trash can around the corner.

We later heard that the men may have followed Dad home from the post office where he stopped at noon, though I never knew whether it was verified. No motive was established for the crime. In 1968 the murderer was found guilty and sentenced to life in prison without parole. He served eleven years.

Gerry, a freshman at nearby Loyola University, was first to arrive on the scene. Here are the memories of that day he shared with me for the first time as I worked on this book.

> One wonders- and I have wondered — how oftentimes "things" just happen to transpire in a way that reduces pain and anguish. My normal routine in coming home from school was to arrive on the side street, Victoria Avenue, where there was access to the garage. But on May 2, 1967, my brother Jim, with whom I shared a ride to school, wanted the car to go to the fraternity house in Manhattan Beach. So, being without a ride, I got a ride home from a friend who dropped me off at the front of the house on 48th Street. I thanked him and went inside not knowing what was transpiring on the other street front.

> The mail already had been delivered because I recall looking through Life magazine. I was doing so when there was a knock on the back door. I went to the door, opened it, and two LA County sheriffs were there. They asked me my name and age (19). They asked me if I was related to Sydney Raycraft and I replied "Yes, he's my father." They then told me they had very bad news and that my father had been murdered. He already had been transported to the morgue.

> I recall going into the house and wondering, "What do I do, where do I go?" I needed to find someone to help me figure out what was going to happen now. My mom and all my siblings — with the exception of Tom who was in Vietnam — were off at school, work or just out and about.

There was no one on whom to rely.

Immediately I thought of one of our closest family friends, the O'Reillys, and I found a set of keys to Tom's MG (he had left it home when he went to Vietnam and my dad loved to drive it) and ran to the garage. To this day I feel guilty about thinking how great it will be to be able to drive the MG, something I didn't normally get to do. I drove – not sure how fast – the mile or so to the O'Reillys house and both Jim and Francis O'Reilly were home. Their children – they had five girls – all were at school. I recall just blurting out, "My dad is dead" and somehow providing them the information I received from the police. They pretty much did the rest though I called my brother Jim at the fraternity house to tell him he had to come home. I recall him resisting the idea so I just had to tell him flat out what had happened. I think I yelled at him. He was heading home.

That afternoon was somewhat of a blur. I recall only pieces. My siblings arriving home (early) from school: Don John from Loyola High School, Phil, Cathy and Mary from St. John the Evangelist Elementary school. Shock and disbelief were the prevailing feelings, with lots of tears. I remember my mom arriving home. Interestingly, with the exception of Tom in Vietnam, Mom was the last to be told. I remember her screaming 'Oh, no; oh, no!' Hugs and tears all around.

Sometime late that afternoon a reporter from the LA Times came by and talked to me and Jim. I can't recall what, if anything I said. Mom loved to tell the story years later about Jim responding to the question 'Would you have any idea who might have done this?' with 'Well, maybe someone in the neighborhood. We had lots of kids and some did not like that' or something along that line.

Those are my memories of that day.

I had always assumed Gerry had to identify Dad's body at the morgue, and that he couldn't talk about it because it was so painful. Now I find out it was our family friends who performed that work of mercy, saving the family from the pain.

I had just begun a job as a social worker for Head Start in Compton, about a forty-minute drive from home. It was the job Dad had assured me I'd get, in our last in-depth conversation.

I was sitting in a child's chair, meeting with teachers and staff of a

Head Start site for which I was responsible when I was called to the phone. Gerry said only to come home immediately, that there was an emergency.

My feelings as I pulled into the driveway near where my father had perished a few hours earlier remain vivid. Seeing Tom's MG parked on the street and assuming an auto accident. I thought, "At least it's not Dad, or that car wouldn't be here."

I walked up the drive to the back door knowing my life was about to change, holding myself back by not wanting to know how. When I entered the kitchen, my friend Kenia and several others were there, acting strangely. They sent me into the TV room. Mom was sitting on the couch, and blurted out something like, "They've killed Dad!" It took a while for me to hear and to comprehend what had happened, from her and the others gathering around.

At the Robert Bly poetry seminar I attended in 2007, I wrote a brief poem about my clearest memory of that day.

Other Insignificant Things / Who or what betrayed me?
In the style of Harry Martinson

A memory of that gray time.
Walking forever up red concrete driveway,
in the muted light of an early May afternoon

Pushed forward by the need to know.
Held back by the sure certainty, that once known,
Nothing would be as it now was.

Dad called our mother
Lod, presumably
from Leocadia, Polish
for Loretta. This
1962 photo shows
them together in
front of their beloved
Crenshaw area home.

This is the only professional photo of the entire family, taken when I was home from Cal
Berkley for Easter break in 1966. From left, front row: John, Cathy, Mom, Su, Mary,
Phil. Back Row: Jim ,Dad, Tom, Gerry and Don.

CHAPTER SIX: DIRECTION

I closed the last chapter walking forever up a red concrete driveway, dreading to find what lay at its end. Now I return to the prior year's letters and the carefree travels of my twenty-two-year-old self. Travel feels like a good metaphor for how this book reveals the dynamic interplay between my own experience and that of others, through the long lens of time.

Letter 9, from 11-year-old Cathy: *"That Boy That Added On Sounded Real Nice"*

Postmarked Aug 1, and received in Rome, Italy, August 6, 1966

Dear Sue,

We got your letter today so mom got these things just now (lightweight mail-grams). I got my hair cut in June but I never told you. At least I don't think so. We go swimming ever day (of coarse). We take round rocks from the rock pile and call them hoarses names then we race them and see who wins. We have jockey standings & I'm Shoemaker. When I went to Balboa I got all sun burned and then I pealed then I went to S.F. It was real fun. Saturday night Jim had a rush party so we went to the movies we saw Help again & around the world under the sea. They were real neat. Europe sounds real neat I wish I could be there. I sitting in the dining room now Mary's taking her temperature & asking me what I'm writing about. We went to play tennis yesterday Dad & I had a set he won of course. Mom was real glad to get a letter from you, she was hoping that she would. When I went to S.F. we went to Chinatown I got a ring for Mary & one me. but it doesn't (fit) so when you come back I'll give it to you. I'm learning to sew now. I'm making a shift now. I'm almost finished it's real fun. I'm fixing Jerry's bed now $1.50 a month. I was sick last week with a sore throat. Mary must of caught it from me. Mom went to the bank to put Mary's 5 dollars in the bank & my 5 dollar *bill. Today Mary & I are going to tennis. It's all right. Maybe when you get back we can have a game.*

That boy that added on sounded real nice ever one laughed when mom read it especially when he said, "Tomorrow we say goodbye and hell *will I be sorry." The summer sure has gone by fast. School is about to start again — terrible just terrible. We saw the sound of music a while ago boy was it good. I'd really like to see it again. We haven't gotten any letter from Tom & we haven't been taping anything on the tape recorder. If you could please send a post card from some & Ireland or some place because I suppose it's real pretty there. Were saving all of your letters. I bet your having a nice time. I've just been swimming most of the time. Jopo likes to listen to the radio theres this one song yellow submarine he loves it. Mom says he's going to turn into a yellow submarine. Running out of room*

Bye, now, Cathy

Cathy, the elder of my two little sisters, was the only sibling to write a separate letter, not as an attachment to one of my parents.

I remember how excited I was when she was born in Concord in 1955, after so long being the only girl in the family. Dad woke me when he took Mom to the hospital in the middle of the night so that I could move downstairs to their room, closer to all the sleeping children. I was always babysitter in charge.

He returned home with the good news, "It's a girl!" They named her after my mother's grandmother, and I suggested they spell her name with K like my best friend, instead of C. Dad told me I could name my children, not his. I loved finding out later how great-grandmother Katherine spelled her name.

Shortly after I left for college at Berkeley in September of 1964, Cathy wrote a letter I still have. Our eldest brother, Tom, had also just left for pilot training in Texas. Cathy's words suggest the bonds between siblings the family fostered.

We just finished clearing out Tom's room and your room. Now we're going to sleep in your room tonight. Of course I'd give your room up if you and Tom were here. . . . Your rooms real nice. I just can't tell you how much I miss you. I can't wait till after this year is over and after 5 years is over because you'll be home and so will Tom. Every time I walk it your room it makes me think of you. And every time I walk into Tom's room it makes me think of Tom. I hope I'm not bothering you. I better go now. PS I would appreciate it if you wrote me. Your my favorite sister.

Cathy's comment in her letter to Rome four years later, "That boy that added on sounded real nice," refers to my July 25, 1966 letter home.

A rare family snapshot from Thanksgiving 1961, two years before Cathy's adoring letter. Front row from Left: Jopo, Mary, Cathy, Phil. Middle: Su, Dad, Mom, Tom. Back: Don, Jim, Gerry.

I wrote from a town called Arenys del Mar, on the Costa del Sol near Barcelona, Spain. We were staying in a 300-bed youth hostel on the beach, full of young travelers like us from many different countries. An "Irish lad" named Carl added the following note to that letter:

Greetings to you Mrs. Raycraft –

You don't know me, but from what I heard you have to be a wonderful woman. A few days ago I had the luck of the Irish to meet your lovely daughter Sue…She's a real colleen, and we really understand each other. Don't you worry about her. She's wonderful, and knows how to mind herself. Anyway no one would ever hurt her. Tomorrow we say Goodbye and hell will I be sorry. But maybe it's just God's will. Next April I go to California, and so we will meet again. Till then, God Bless, Carl

When I began this project, I discovered among the letters a card I'd received from Carl at Christmas 1966, sharing a big decision:

> *When I left that little town in Spain I went south and after three weeks I decided to return to home. Sue, do you remember me telling you about always trying to find myself, you recall me saying I wanted so much to be a doctor, and my parents wishing I take over Pa's business. Sue, I have decided to become a priest, and now I feel my life is to have a meaning – to give my life to God and to other people, that is what I always wanted, and it took me till now to realize it, to meet a girl named Sue. I write to you to tell you this, as you were one of the few people who ever influenced me in the ways that matter most. I just want you to know why I will not be calling to see you next summer as I said. Sue you will I am sure understand, and you are the only person I really care to do so. As far as I can determine, one never knows just what's around the corner for him.*

Carl's cryptic closing sentence pretty much sums it up: we never really know, do we? And yet we stay so busy preparing for what we think it will be that we often miss what is going on right in front of us. That lesson is one my observant father worked hard to teach his scattered daughter.

One experience clearly illustrates this dynamic of his parenting. Just before leaving for Berkeley in the fall of 1964, I organized a group of friends to leaflet cars at the Los Angeles Greek Theater. Our flyer endorsed a fair housing initiative that was on the November ballot. My friend Kenia asked if her young brother, Diego, could stay at my house while she joined the leafletting crew.

The only car we had among our group was too small to hold us all, so we left it and drove my parents' station wagon. Diego panicked among strangers and cried for much of the evening. His parents had no car, and I forgot to leave the keys to the emergency car, so my parents couldn't take him home. Because cell phones didn't exist in those days, they had to contend with the drama and were not happy when I returned home several hours later.

I vividly recall the discussion Dad and I had the next day, down to the detail of where we sat together on the lawn near the pool. He pointed out that my focus on others had created problems in my own home for which I must take responsibility.

My chief concern, he told me, should be attention to those closest to me, before I worried about "saving the rest of the world." Twenty years later that well-remembered conversation inspired "Direction," one of the first poems I wrote as I began the work of hearing my voice, something that is essential for self-healing.

Direction

I grew up in an exceptional family – nine children, Mom and Dad,
We'd pray together and play together, brown eyes against blue.
My father had a guiding role, and when I was troubled or mad,
He'd take me aside and ask, "Don't you see what you do?"

You take care of all the world, with a scattered mind,
While here at home your mother hurts, your own family cries."
And I'd reply, "Dad, that's true, how could I be so blind"?
I did not see the need within, right before my eyes.

Then his path turned, Death carved him from our side,
And left a gaping hole, from which I chose to hide.
I filled it with memories, fear, and self-denial,
Cementing it with more pain, when my brother Jim too died.

My focus stayed on others; I feared to go within.
My dad taught half a lesson, the rest I had to learn.
By challenging the myth of the strong external hand
Church and Home and Culture have given to the man.

For many years I denied how I felt about those deaths;
I grew to be a woman who avoided speaking truth.
Taking care of all the world, while sacrificing self
Taught me to stay unworthy of knowing my own depths.

Slowly I grew stronger and began to read the signs,
To leave others their own struggles, refuse to make them mine.
I took the time to heal myself, starting deep within,
To release my buried feelings, to find my voice again.

My core belief was brought to light, its hold on me was freed,
Not only through the lost father-guide could I really know me.
I am a strong and vibrant woman, whose direction becomes clear,
When I look inside, listen well, and let go all the fear.

CHAPTER SEVEN: REALLY NEAT GUYS AND A SWEDISH GIRL

Letter 10, from 12½-year-old Philip: *"I Hope You Are Having Fun And Come Back Soon"*

Postmarked August 1, and Received in Rome, Italy, on August 6, 1966

Dear Sue,

How are you? I haven't written lately because I have been busy in summer school, but Friday we finished. As a means of evaluating our progress, they administered a standardized test for English & Math. I received my results the next day and I learned that I was #1 in English and about #10 in Math. In the total score I was ranked in the first five. Two weeks ago, Steve Kristovich slept over. We had a fine time going swimming and playing Rummy 500. He is improving from the illness, but still is lying in bed. This week we started racing rolling rocks. The one that goes the farthest is the winner. We race practically everyday and have lots of fun. I hope you are having fun and come back soon. Your brother, Phil

Letter 11, from Dad: *"Hope You Continue To Meet Really Neat Guys"*

Dear Sue,

I expect 1967 will bring an influx of foreign visitors to Los Angeles and that a goodly no. of them will find their way to our pad – all this in the way of response to your impact on Europe. We are happy that you are faring so well and having a good time. If the Spanish are so friendly, you just may decide to stay in Italy when you get there. Also, if you have put on a little weight already, the Italian diet may be a further step up.

Are you going on to Greece? Don't recall your mentioning much about that since you left the U.S. Also, what happened to the plan to visit Ireland?

All are well here except for a virus infection with Mary — nothing serious. July was a perfect month for weather in L.A. — sorry you couldn't make it.

Donald spent a few days in the mtns with a couple of friends and parents of one of them. Returned very impressed and <u>very</u> dirty.

Jim is now at Hamilton AFB for summer camp training-ROTC. Not much news from Tom but what we get is usually interesting and indicative of progress in learning to fly!

We had the ADG rush party here the night before Jim left for Hamilton. Looked like a "slim pickins" prospect list. Guess they're concentrating on quality rather than quantity. Also most of the "really good guys" have grade problems.

So far I've avoided starting the living room renovation but have made considerable progress with the yard work — with assistance from Don and John. Just wait till you get home and try to settle down to the relative quiet of life here. I hope the contrast is a welcome change and perhaps by then it will be.

I hope you like Rome — I should think it would be the most fascinating place of all. It must just reek of history & Christianity. Hope you continue to meet "really neat guys." Take care, have fun, God bless you — in reverse order!

Love, Dad

When I first typed this letter for the book, I couldn't resist calling to share it with Phil's wife, Tammy. She marveled at how much he sounded like their then five-year-old son, Donovan.

Dad alludes in this letter to our "impact on Europe," trusting I will "continue to meet 'really neat guys'." I recorded our adventures in a tiny calendar and wrote home about many of them. We drank with Irish boys in Belgium on July 8, met "typical Spanish boys" selling chiclet (gum) from a motorbike in Toledo July 19, and camped with French guys on the beach near Barcelona July 24.

Occasionally Cathy, Dale, and I split up. One of us would hitchhike with someone we'd met; then we'd regroup at the next youth hostel. In my July 12 letter from Madrid, I explain that I'd joined up with a young British traveler to visit Lourdes. While I knew going to a famous Catholic shrine would gain their approval, I can't believe how much I shared in that letter.

I describe our visiting Lourdes late on July 11, then walking on to the coastal town of Anglet, near Biarritz. Arriving too late to get into the youth hostel, we found a local park where I slept on the grass with a view of the ocean below.

I tell of being awakened by a policeman yelling in French that I was sleeping dangerously close to the cliff. I must have wanted so badly for my Catholic parents to know I visited Lourdes, I failed to censor the late night arrival and unorthodox sleeping arrangements.

In my July 25 letter from Arenys del Mar in Spain, I share one of our most unexpected encounters. Here's how I describe the experience of meeting a young Swedish girl in Barcelona.

> On the morning before we left for here I was talking to the girl in the bed next to me – she's from Sweden. I mentioned we were leaving, and right away she asks, 'Can I go with you?'
>
> She was supposed to meet her traveling companions, a pair of twin boys, on the beach in Barcelona but had missed them and was alone and really miserable. Only eighteen, just darling and really nice. So I said sure and she's here with us now and is going to stay till she meets her friends further on in Spain, hopefully. We're really glad we found her, and I'm sure she's glad too.

Her name was Marianne and she traveled with us for a week, from the coast of Spain, through France and into Italy. As we traveled, we would stop passing kids, show them a photo and ask if they'd seen the twins. We found someone who had, standing on the street outside the Genoa youth hostel. A joyous reunion ensued, followed by tearful good-byes as Marianne left to travel home with them.

Marianne and the twins enjoy a street moment before she lost them on a Barcelona beach. Is that a kitten?

I found the above photograph as well as Marianne's mournful letter to us in Hamburg that September, after we'd sent a postcard to her home in Sweden. She was bored in her small village and yearned to be with us again enjoying "the wonderful spirit that you meet when you are out hitchhiking." She'd told her parents about meeting us and, as I did with my parents, glossed over many of the details.

They thought she'd spent most of her travels in the protective company of three older Americans, rather than with the twins and their friends drinking Guinness. This story of rescuing a young Swedish girl and helping her find her lost traveling companions received excellent feedback in my letters from home.

The theme of meeting boys permeates my letters from London, Paris, Madrid, Florence, Vienna, a German army base, and Bergen in Norway. I tell of hanging out with "one-half the American fleet" August 6–8 in Rome, Italian soldiers on a motorcycle in Florence August 10, and a Polish boy in Yugoslavia August 13. We spent the next night "in the field with American boys." With no hanky panky!

And for the grand finale, on August 15, I fell in love with Fritz, an Austrian ski instructor in front of Vienna's famous cathedral. Together we visited the castle that inspired the author of Sleeping Beauty, which turned out to be the perfect metaphor for the experience.

When you're twenty-two and far from all you've known, that's how it goes. Thinking back on how innocent it all was by today's standards makes me laugh. In between meeting all these members of the opposite sex, the three of us never missed Sunday Mass in an assortment of churches, from cathedrals to army chapels, the entire trip.

In my August 8 letter from Florence, I share receiving the Pope's blessing at his summer residence and how a priest in Rome waved me away from the communion rail, presumably for wearing a sleeveless blouse.

By the midpoint of my trip, I'd begun talking about how good the quiet of home would sound, and how heavy my pack was feeling. We didn't have fancy backpacks with aluminum frames common today; ours were simple square-shaped canvas affairs with no frame, shoulder or waist pads. And for the entire first month, we always wore skirts while hitchhiking (called "auto stop" in Europe in the 60s) as we'd heard that would help us get rides.

In mid-August, I write from Vienna about leaving my purse by the side of the road when a driver picked us up. We asked him to backtrack and found that the local police had it, with my passport and money intact. Why I assumed my parents wouldn't know we were hitchhiking from that tale astounds me.

It's not surprising that Dad starts this letter anticipating an influx of foreign visitors. He also mentions for the first time the living room project, calling it a "restoration," which involved more work than the simple patching and painting Mom wanted. "So far I've avoided getting started," he quips.

Exploring the letters I've kept from both sides of the Atlantic, I feel like a miner unearthing gold nuggets. The words seem tangible and contain something of the writer's life force in their simple directness.

Reading and rereading them, I feel Dad's presence in his shades of sarcasm, Mom's in her attention to detail. Between Dad's scientific mind, and Mom's double Virgo horoscope, both were thoroughly organized in all they did. Perhaps my scattered approach to life manifests a need to rebel, or at least to be different from what I felt my orderly parents expected of me.

Sharing these letters has been a gift to myself. I've enjoyed introducing the youthful, free spirit I have always been to the nieces, nephews, and grandchildren who have only known me as a boringly mature "older woman."

Dad's well-crafted letter inspires me to close this chapter with something I've treasured all these years. When he retired from Shell in 1966, his buddies transferring to its Eastern District threw him a retirement party. Don McKenna wrote words to the tune of the Whiffenpoof song, which they all sang together after many toasts and probably in decidedly drunken tones. One of those friends gave me a copy after Dad's death, which I pass on here.

Here's to you Dad, in the words, and long-ago voices of your buddies. I love to think I may have inherited your flare for words, and intend the magic of your talking be a gift of my book.

May Infinity be, if not explained, honored by your presence! I love you.

The Raycraft Fan Song
(To the tune of the Whiffenpoof song)

From the bar rooms down at Torrance
To the golf course in Palm Springs
To the Stamford District Office of the East

Sing the Raycraft fans assembled
With their glasses raised on high
And the magic of their singing is a beast.

Oh the magic of Sid's talking
Will be missed by one and all
And we'll surely have to realign our plans.

We will reminisce of Raycraft
The "Introduction Kid"
Cause there's no one who can give a speech like Sid.

We're poor little fans, and look what they did
     Baa   Baa   Baa
The talks we'll now hear, won't be from Sid
     Baa   Baa   Baa

Fellow listeners, what's our destiny
Raycraft's speeches explained infinity
Who else can confuse us such as he
     Baa   Baa   Baa

CHAPTER EIGHT: CONNECTING

Letter 12, from Mom: *"Don't Worry About What People Say"*

Postmarked August 13, received in Munich, Germany, August 24, 1966; it arrived August 17

Dear Sue,

I'll write first today. We received your letter from Florence today & enjoyed it very much. Don't worry about what people say – at least you're having a lot of experiences that you wouldn't have had (even going the traditional way). Besides, I tell everyone you girls are really roughing it. My sister Marie is going to Europe in Sept for 22 days on a tour. They are going to Eng, France, Germany, Switzerland, Liechtenstein, Austria, Italy & Spain. Perhaps you could drop her a note if you'll be in one of those places around the 5th of Sept. Kind of impossible tho – because I don't know where she will be but perhaps you'll meet by chance.

Mailed a tape to Tom this morning. If all goes well we're hoping to see him next weekend on his cross-country. Salazar (one of the instructors & a brother of Ben Aranda's wife) spoke up to go with Tom – so in this way both can see their families. Sounds pretty definite except for weather conditions & that no one can do anything about. Did you get the letter I wrote in Barcelona about Dad & I planning on going down for his graduation on Oct 26th? We plan to visit Dad's sister in San Antonio also. Figured we could count on you to keep the home fires burning. You'll probably be pretty contented just staying home.

Jerry went to Arrowhead for the weekend so the 5 oldest are all gone. Jim's written several times & his letters are so different from yours & Tom's. Very brief & right to the point – such as "I won the Butterfly race our swim meet," "We marched for 4 hrs," etc. He's getting enough to eat anyhow. Jerry had to take a test to get into R.O & was accepted.

Said it was very hard. One of his friends didn't make it.

Mary was sick all last week with the virus – it settled in her chest & I had to take her to the Dr. & she had a lot of medicine, but is ok now. The 3 O'Reilly girls spent the nite here & now they are playing house. Phil & Don are out racing rocks.

Sue do you remember Mr. Smith at Shell? You used to go in & talk with him when you worked at the Data Center. He had a heart attack July 10th but we didn't hear about it until the end of July – no one called & Dad wrote – he couldn't have any company. Dad called Tues nite (the 9th) to find out how he was & here he had died the Tues before & was buried on Fri. & we didn't even know. What a shock! Steve Kristovich is back in the hospital – they operated on him & found an infection – almost like an enormous boil (it finally came to a head) so they are encouraged to know what it was. He should be ok now but is still in the hospital. What do you think of your smart brother Phil? John is at Balboa today – went with the Ridgleys – Tom Trapp is in town this week & next, so he's been doing more than sitting on his "butt."

I started a little sewing. I had made Cathy a 2-piece bathing suit & am making one for Mary now. Also each a dress – same pattern & same material except different colors. Can't seem to get too much sewing done tho. Tried to teach Cathy some sewing. We made her a shift – she did all the straight seams & I finished it up. One thing she did learn was threading the machine – the thread kept coming out all the time.

Wally Mattingly took the scholarship to Cal in Berkeley. His girl friend is going to Dominican College in San Raphael so I'm sure that was one of his reasons for going there.

Had another sinus headache this weekend & lost 1 ½ days – it was on my left side, now I feel it coming on my right side.

Mrs. Tassano called last week – told me Briggie Woulfe ran off to Reno & got married last spring. Msgr. Hennessey won't bless their marriage until he thinks they are sure it will last. Saw Sister John Michael (she had Jim in the 2nd grade). Remember we named Jopo after her & Paul Joseph. She is so funny. Wanted to see pictures of everyone so we went back in the evening to see her. She kept telling the others how darling Sue was & how cute I had the kids dressed. She was sure funny. Asked me if I ever had any more girls, so I took Cathy & Mary back with me.

Dad came too & she said he hadn't changed a bit — just as young as ever. It was 12 years since we've seen her & she remembered so many people in Concord etc.

Guess I wrote enuff for one time. I got some more of these letters, so perhaps others will write too.

Dad still is home — goes to the Commodities market every day — sold some & made some money. Hasn't even started the living room — I wonder if he'll get it done by next June. According to everyone, they are all coming out for our 25ᵗʰ anniversary.

Love, Mother

I am thrilled to have in writing my mother's telling me not to worry about what anyone says! I had written in my August 8 letter from Florence should any of her friends meet me on the road, they'd pretend they didn't know me. I could tell they'd figured out by now that hitchhiking was the "nontraditional" mode of travel to which I referred in that letter.

I was surprised both parents seemed to take it so casually. I figured they assumed it was commonplace in Europe, which was true in 1966. We met other hitchhiking youth, though never a group of three doing it for such an extended period.

How funny that after saying it would be impossible to plan to meet Aunt Marie she adds that perhaps it will happen by chance.

Mom visiting a nun who had taught her children a decade earlier in another city, then returning for a second visit with Dad and later additions to the family reveals the value our parents placed on relationships. They modeled and passed on to their offspring the ability to create and honor deep personal connections.

I'm sure the nuns appreciated this woman whose devotion to motherhood modeled what they taught as the Catholic ideal. Unlike her eldest daughter, who became a mother through my husband's children, she seemed born to be one. I bet Sister John Michael still remembered Mom's Christmas candy. Here too is the proof that Jopo was named John Paul after two of his mother's favorite nuns.

As in all her letters, not only does Mom detail each of her own children's activities, she comments on one friend's illness, another's scholarship and a third's wedding (or lack thereof in Catholic circles). Her sharing the specifics of the death of Dad's co-worker touched me. Dad comments on that same death in his next letter; they shared memories of their friend, and both remembered I liked him.

In the same spirit, my letters home capture the genuine interest and care shown us by strangers in every country we visited. I knew all my readers enjoyed hearing that.

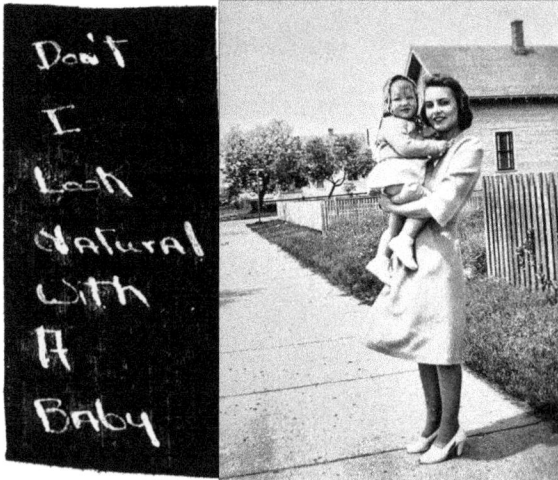

This is twenty-eight year old Loretta Wujcik, my mother, holding her first-born niece, Barbara Jean Dedick.

The captioned photograph was among those she saved in an album never shown to her children and almost thrown away.

In addition to natives, we met many Americans, military personnel stationed abroad or tourists like us. Local drivers picked up three backpack-laden young women, squeezed them and their luggage into impossibly small cars, and delivered them to safe destinations. Several invited us to spend a night in their homes, and one businessmen treated us to a room and lavish meal in a remote Spanish castle.

Occasionally someone would take too good care of us. I write in a letter home about a pensione manager in Rome who, wouldn't even let us out of our room to talk to the American boys across the hall, saying, "Italy is different than America."

I do remember feeling that because we were out walking the streets, we must be fair game for male attention, mostly in Italy and to some degree in Spain. That assumption and the hassles it caused us felt more annoying than dangerous. Our freedom was compromised to a degree we weren't used to, and I returned home with a greater appreciation for the American male. In my letter from Rome I describe it thus:

> *We went to Vatican City — climbed 537 steps to the top of St. Peter's dome, where I took a picture of 3 Italian marines — quite taken with themselves these Italians. Also persistent. We'd heard so much about Italian men and it's all true. They won't leave girls alone — especially blonds, so it's worse for Dale and Cathy. But it really gets annoying because you can never relax. That's why we turned to the Marines — met some really nice ones.*

Another gift of this journey was greater appreciation for the art and architecture of other ages than I had learned growing up in California. And in the retrospective glance from over fifty years, the best gift of my coming-of-age voyage is gratitude for my own home and family.

Mom mentions the living room renovation again in this letter; Dad had alluded to it in the preceding one. Though Mom wanted to have it done, she also dreaded it, almost as if she knew it would always remind us what remained unfinished as life went on past the idyllic days of the summer of '66.

CHAPTER NINE: FLIT AND FLOURISH

Letter 13, from 9 ½ -year-old Mary: *"We Woke Up At 7:30 And Had a Peaceful Day"*

Postmarked August 15, and received August 26 in Munich, Germany

Dear Sue,

This year Cathy and I are going to take mom out for lunch. I almost have 3 dollars and Cathy has 75 cents. I put $5.00 in the bank and I had $2.00 interest so now I have $27.44. I've been going to day camp which is every other day. Laurie O'Rielly or mom usually takes us. We sing songs, play games, and crafts, and other things. Friday the 3 O'Riellys, me and Billy did a puppet show The Princess and the Pea, Little Red Ridinghood, and a song. Elizabeth, Marie and Laurie slept over the other night. We stayed up until 11:00 watching Man from U.N.C.L.E. it was the Batcave Affair. Then we went upstairs where we where going to go to sleep. We were noisy so dad said outloud those O'Reilly's better start packing then everyone was silent. Cathy went into the other room because of the commosion. We woke up at 7:30 and had a peaceful day until they left. Good Bye Now: Mary

Letter 14 from Dad: *"Well, Dear Daughter, I Hope You Continue To Flit And Flourish, For Now Is The Time And Wherever You Are Is The Place."*

Dear Sue,

We enjoyed your letter from Rome. I'm also getting quite a kick reading Mary's composition above. I can just see you and Dale going down the street in Genoa peering into peoples' faces and then referring to your snapshot in search of the "lost Scandinavians."

I hope you find Germany as enjoyable as Spain and Italy. Have a stein

of beer for me in Munich. Will you get to Vienna – I've heard that is the friendliest fun spot in all of Europe. You have to hit the gay spots so we can get our vicarious "enjoys."

Things are going smoothly at home – knock, knock – just a couple more weeks till school starts and none of the children appear eager to return. Jim is surviving summer camp at Hamilton and has written a couple of priceless, cryptic notes.

Cathy is starting to do the dishes and Mom says to tell you she is making excellent progress. Philip is resting on his summer school laurels. We are expecting Tom for an overnight next weekend. He'll be making his cross-country check flight in the company of Ben Aranda's cousin – who is an instructor at Laughlin AFB.

It was nice to hear that American marines are a better choice than Latin Lovers. The pensione mgr must judge everybody's morals by the conduct of the Italian male. You surely entered Italy in a "state of ignorance" if you were unaware of the taboo on bare arms at Mass. I'm surprised the priest gave you communion.

Fr. O'Reilly is long back from his European trip – had a nice time – best weather in a long time – he always asks about you.

Mom said she would mention to you that Ken Smith died of a heart attack. Poor soul won't have to fight the frustrations of Shell and the freeways any longer.

Well, dear daughter, I hope you continue to flit and flourish, for now is the time and wherever you are is the place.

I would wish you could get to Ireland but it doesn't sound like you'll make it.

Give my worst to the Berlin wall.

Love, Dad

Mary's short letter is priceless. Nearly three weeks before Mom's birthday she's planning how to celebrate, and enlisting her siblings to join her. It seems all the Raycrafts excel at organizing others.

These two letters provide more detailed descriptions of day-to-day life in the remarkable place I called home, from both a child and a parent's perspective. The youngest child at only nine speaks of having a peaceful day. And in her slumber party description, she conveys the respect bordering on fear our friends felt for our father.

Her mention of watching "The Batcave Affair" on TV reminds me of one of my favorite Dad stories from when I was just a couple years older, probably ten or eleven. We'd pay a dime (or was it a quarter?) to go to the downtown Concord Saturday Matinee, where I fell in love with a series called "Blackhawk."

Like Batman, Blackhawk hid in a cave and confronted evil. I'd come home from the film and tell Dad all about it, trying to convince him he should see it with us some Saturday. "Blackhawk, it's real good, you'd like it," was apparently my oft-repeated phrase, for he seized on it as the perfect metaphor for my impulse to try to influence others. Whenever he caught me trying to talk anyone into doing something I wanted them to do, he'd chime in, "Blackhawk, real good, you'd like it."

I have shared the story many times as evidence of my father's keen understanding of his children's personalities and characters, and his sometimes sarcastic intervention.

My recollection is that rather than feeling offended when he "Blackhawked" me, I'd step back and think about whether the person really would like it. His comment pushed me to understand my tendencies and compulsions, for which I have been forever grateful to my observant father.

My husband Larry shares many of Dad's qualities, which might explain some of our attraction. Driving to Concord in the early eighties, he pulled off the freeway when he saw a sign reading *BLACKHAWK*. Directional arrows led to a new housing development by that name, with huge houses in various stages of construction. "Blackhawk, you'd like it," he quipped.

This letter of Dad's is one of my favorites. It opens with his comments on the story I'd shared in my July 25 letter about the "Swedish girl" we adopted in Spain and helped reconnect with her friends in Italy. I describe that experience in Chapter 7.

My father calls me "dear daughter" here, and communicates the vicarious enjoyment my hitting the "gay spots" of Europe gave him. From advising me that "Now is the time and wherever you are is the place to flit and flourish," to drinking a stein of beer for him in Munich, to his lecture about my state of ignorance regarding bare arms in Italian churches, this letter represents Sid Raycraft as father.

One of my most cherished memories of his fatherly advice comes from a conversation just a couple weeks before he died. During several months of job hunting in early 1967, I met an acquaintance who asked me what I was doing. I came home and shared with my father how embarrassed I was to tell someone who knew me as the exalted student body president from high school, that four years and a college degree later, I couldn't even find a job.

At the time, Dad had been unemployed for almost a full year, and I wondered how he handled situations like this. He told me that he had a plan, and he was right on track with it. Instead of worrying about what others think, I should focus on my plan for my life.

Dad went on to say that most people, especially casual acquaintances like the girl I'd met, really don't care about what we are doing, they're merely curious. The only ones who should concern us are members of our immediate small circle, mostly family and a few close friends.

"In fewer than 25 years, no one except family and those few friends will even remember we were here," he shocked me by saying.

Understanding my concern about employment, he concluded with advice on job hunting, suggesting I not believe all I hear. When interviewers say you're not qualified for a job, they mean they don't need your particular skills. When the right job opens up, you'll know that it's right for you because it's part of your plan. And you'll get it.

What my father communicated to me as we cooked lunch on the kitchen stove that April afternoon has gifted me his wisdom throughout my life. I have shared it countless times in many situations; it always reminds me of my father's commitment to living his truth and teaching his children to live theirs.

Dad made the plan to which he referred when he refused Shell's offer of a transfer to New York as the price of his continued employment. Mom had agreed to give him a full year to explore options for supporting the family. He and I had this conversation as that year was coming to its end. These letters to his eldest daughter as she wandered across Europe capture the freedom his plan created.

I love this photo of my parents at the University of Minnesota's Minneapolis campus. I feel Dad's focus on his life plan as they stand directly on a path symbolic of the one upon which they had embarked.

The quality of my father's life during that single year seems to me unmatched in his twenty years as a chemical engineer with a few weeks annual vacation, often coinciding with the birth of a new baby. I believe he lived it as consciously and joyfully as I have ever witnessed a life lived. As if he knew it would be his last.

Dad refers to Vienna as the "friendliest fun spot in all of Europe" in this letter. Like Cathy's loving "Sound of Music," in the previous one, his comment foreshadows the importance that particular city held for me. Later on the very day this letter was postmarked I met Fritz on the steps of its famous cathedral.

He mentions his former co-worker Ken Smith, whom I learned in Mom's most recent letter had died, referring to him as a poor soul who would no longer have to fight the frustrations of Shell or freeway driving.

In his letters Dad says little about his activities, always focusing on the kids. When I returned, I learned he was experimenting in the garage with his favorite chile recipe, exploring mass producing and marketing it, much to Mom's dismay.

My father modeled invaluable lessons in 1966 and '67, as he played with possibilities and tried things deemed unusual and risky by the world around him. His example has inspired me to be willing to risk the disapproval and even ridicule of others.

And the extra time he had that year to notice his children, play tennis or attend Mass with them, help with homework, plan and organize maintenance jobs, and simply be present in their lives was a priceless gift.

CHAPTER TEN: RICK RACK AND PEA SOUP

Letter 15, from Mom: *"There Goes That Pessimistic Mother Again"*

Postmarked August 19 and received in Munich, Germany, August 26

Dear Sue,

It's dinnertime & I'm already to eat but the fellow is putting in a new drier – what a time to come. Anyhow we've never gotten a new drier because we couldn't find one to fit in the space. The other day Dad went down to a Maytag place to get a part for my washer & saw this one that would fit. It's yellow but that was immaterial at this point & we did get a good buy. At the same time I got a call from Father O'looney – he just got back from Mexico & was leaving for Northern Calif – wasn't sure where he would be stationed but said to be sure to have you girls write to his sister's place in San Rafael – so please do – otherwise he won't think I told you. The man was trying to call the shop – it was a mess & I had to cut the call short – what a mess.

Cathy is sick again – sore throat – temp & very disgusted. She makes me feel like it's my fault that she's sick.

Talked to Dale's mother today – she's been back in King City – Dale's stepfather's father is real sick – was real bad during the weekend but seems to have gotten better. Cece is supposed to get her ring tomorrow.

We had pea soup tonite & left overs – Dad, Jerry & Don are trying to get the drier in place now – so I'll try & finish this & get it off. I want to sew tonite – I put a time limit on the dresses I'm making Cathy & Mary (otherwise I won't get it done). Couldn't sleep last nite so came down & sewed little rick rack on the dress – went to bed at 3.

We've gotten quite a few letters from Jim – the one today has been newsier than the others. Evidently he's doing pretty well – he was one of 2 cadets interviewed by the representative of the Inspector General. I don't know what it means but it's impressive. He claims he's doing real well, especially in athletics but says the rest of the flight is lousy & very unathletic. Saw John Tassano last weekend & Plans to spend a few days in Concord when he's thru with summer camp.

We're all looking forward to Tom's cross-country & hope it's this weekend. It's been 8 mo. since we've seen him & it seems longer. It's almost 3 mo. since I've seen you & it seems like years. The time is going by fast.

I reread your last letter & I got a charge out of your millionaire Irish friend – really how do you know – he could tell you lots of stories. There goes that pessimistic mother again – I can almost hear you saying that.

We went to a Dodger game with the Ryans last Mon nite & out to dinner with the O'Reilly's the following nite – so now we're ready to stay home for a while.

Saw Sister Michelle Marie at church Mon. & she's going to St. Thomas in SF, the same place as Jack's sister is at. They were going up together. I told you I saw Jack at Jonie's wedding but only said "hello." Mrs. Kane is working so I haven't seen or talked to her.

Tom Trapp was down from Daly City for about 12 days & spent about 3 days with us. It was nice having him – he's no trouble at all.

I'm really pulling at straws trying to fill up this letter – there's nothing much more I can tell you.

Phil hasn't been too hot this summer – he had a lousy July & that's usually a good mo. for him. He's been serving a lot. By the way Father O'Reilly asked what happened to you? Are you planning on going to Ireland? Other thing I wanted to ask – do you get around by bus or bicycle? Also have those arnell dresses come in handy or haven't you been able to use them?

Oh yes, Cathy has taken over the dish washing. I've been helping her put things away but she does most of the work.

Guess I'll wash a batch of clothes & dry them. The old one was tearing clothes, etc. & it was getting harder & harder for Dad to fix it.

Haven't done anything about the living room yet – thought it would be all done by the time you'd be home but I'll be glad if it's done by next June. Lucky I'm not too demanding – ha?

Well Sue – have fun. When you get this you'll only have 1 more month & that will go fast.

Love & kisses, Mother

My favorite Mom letter, this epitomizes Loretta Raycraft. Like Dad calling me "dear daughter" in his of a few days earlier, this one holds my mother's "love and kisses" and reminds me how important I was in her life.

She describes the repairman who arrived at dinnertime to install a new clothes dryer and needed to use the phone at the exact moment my friend called. In spite of the confusion, she took a message which she rather urgently conveys to me in this letter.

Fifty years later I still see her putting dinner on hold to start writing to me while waiting for the dryer installation. Then finishing the letter after caring for a sick child; this was the night before Phil was rushed to the hospital. All this while planning the time to sew the girls' dresses after staying up until 3 AM the previous night sewing rick rack on those dresses.

She sewed her clothes and made nearly all those her three daughters wore growing up. In different cities and decades, she served as president of two parents' groups, called "Mother's Clubs" in those days. At St. John' in LA, she starred as Granny in the group's production of "Hollywood Hillbillies" in 1965 or 66, in a costume she made herself.

Mom wrote nine of the nineteen letters sent to me during my three months of travel, though surely she was busier than anyone else. It all came under the heading of Mother's Work, a job she performed with skill and determination for most of her life.

Have I mentioned she knew how to stand on her head? On the rare occasions she'd come out to join us on a summer evening, her wide-eyed children would stop playing on the lawn and try to emulate this unexpected motherly skill, which she could do for quite an extended period.

Uncharacteristically self-observant in this letter, she responds to a story in one of my letters that she can hear me calling her a "pessimistic mother" for doubting my Irish friend is a millionaire.

Referring to Dad's reluctance to begin the living room remodel, she quips, "Good thing I'm not too demanding—Ha?"

Mom holds her sixth child, John Paul, in this Thanksgiving 1952 snapshot, probably taken with a Brownie camera. My dress was part of a "Mother-Daughter outfit" because it matched one she made for herself, though only mine had the hat. Check out the black gloves the two eldest boys wore, decades before Michael Jackson.

Her "demands" were usually requests, and rather than hold out for them, she was likely to retreat into quiet resignation, tinged with a bit of blame likely to produce some guilt in the other. We all learned to live with some "Good old Catholic guilt."

Mom closed this letter with the hope that Dad would finish repairing the living room by the following June. In retrospect, what prevented it makes that more poignant, as does her mentioning a meal that had long been a family favorite, pea soup.

Mom lived alone for the last two decades of her life, after losing her husband and sending off the last of her nine children. In her simple home on the street I call "walking in the light" (Calle de Andalucia) in the Redondo Beach hills, she created a balance to her early life of serving others.

Steeped in solitude, Mom enjoyed reading two daily newspapers. She hung out with lifelong friends, including her companion and escort to social events, George Steinmetz. Visiting her children and grandchildren and welcoming them in her home were priorities. She continued her lifelong love of sewing and specialized in Halloween costumes for the grandkids. Whenever Mom couldn't sleep in the early morning hours, she'd get up and sew, a habit developed early in her life.

During her Calle de Andalucia years, we corresponded regularly. Like the letters in this book, she filled her later ones with glimpses of daily life and interactions with her children and friends. Seldom did she share reminiscences or regrets.

She mentioned in a 1994 letter that she no longer made pea soup because she could only find split peas in the stores. When I discovered whole peas at a Marin County farmer's market, I sent her several pounds.

I had also recently mailed her copies of some of my poems about my healing around Dad and Jim's deaths, as a step toward early work on this book. In her letter thanking me for the peas, she talks about the pea soup she last made for Dad.

On May 2, 1967, my mother was finishing her year of service as president of the St. John the Evangelist Mother's Club, and planning the traditional luncheon to welcome next year's officers. She spent the day with her friend Vanni, visiting Busch Gardens in the San Fernando Valley as a potential venue.

Driving home, she passed the cemetery during a funeral procession. She recalls feeling grateful it was no one she knew personally. When she arrived home, friends were gathering, and she learned that her husband had been murdered while she was eating lunch with her friend.

Over the years she had occasionally shared her memories of that day. She went into detail about them in the tapes Tom and I helped her make several decades later, which we completed in the months before her death.

Some of her words in that 1994 letter jumped off the page for me. By adding just a few words, they became a complete poem.

Mom's Pea Soup

I was cooking pea soup the day Dad was killed,
in that deep well on our electric stove.
I left it simmering and wrote him a note
to check it when he got home.

I got the recipe from his mother
when I was still a young bride;
she said it was how the French cooked it,
that only whole peas made it right.

He used to say it was his favorite meal,
with homemade bread and sliced onions.
I'd made it so often in twenty-five years,
the whole family had learned to love it.

I often wondered what happened
to that pot of pea soup on the stove.
Friends came in and took over,
probably dumped it, I don't know.

So many things changed forever that day,
while so many have stayed just the same.
I can't make pea soup without thinking
of that last meal I cooked for your dad.

Loretta Raycraft taught her family how to move beyond loss and live in the light of the present moment. Focused on raising her children as a single mother, at fifty-seven she enrolled in a clerical skills class to learn bookkeeping; she supported herself for the years before qualifying for social security.

Our mother gave her children the small gifts of memory-making recipes and the large ones of courage in the face of sudden loss and dramatic change. She blessed everyone who shared her life and love.

CHAPTER ELEVEN: DREAMS AND DRAMA

Letter 16, from 11-year-old Cathy: *"On Mom's Birthday Mary And I Took Mom And Dad Out For Lunch"*

Postmarked Sept 11 in Los Angeles, received Sept 14, 1966, in Bergen, Norway

Dear Sue,

How is everything in Europe? School has just started & now I wish it would end. I have Sr. Mercedes. (She's so old) We take Spanish this year. (el padre y la madre) it means father and mother. Thursday I slept over my friend Loretta's. I also slept over Fri. night. Sat. morning we went hoarse back riding. My horses name was Peewee & Loretta's horses name was Sheen (something like that) Boy it was fun. But my horse bit Loretta's horse. She almost fell off. On Mom's birthday Mary & I took Mom & Dad out for lunch. Dad & Phil came to. It was real fun. We paid for the bill. I can't think of anything to say so I'll say goodbye.

Unsigned

Letter 17, from Dad: *"Perhaps You Can Wield a Beneficial Influence"*

Dear Sue,

From the foregoing presentation by Cathy, you can see that she is not a very active participant in the quest for knowledge. Mary is worse. Perhaps you can wield a beneficial influence when you get home since they must think that you are quite a wheel in the big machine.

There was not much point in concerning you about Philip at the time of his attack, and, now that it's over, we can give you the brief details. It came on suddenly – he had a bad night on a Thursday – shots, "pozzitories," pills, to the limit of allowances – and he just got by. So, the next night when he started down hill even faster than the night before, we called the Dr. at 10pm, and it was decided to hospitalize him.

It was a fortunate decision, since he was <u>very</u> bad for the next two days, and then gradually came out of it. He's now ok (for Phil) and ornery as ever.

Mom says to tell you Wayne called tonight and asked us to inform you that he will <u>not</u> be picking you up in New York. Car condition, his other plans, etc. are all against it, but I believe the car is the determining factor. I guess you can get out your U.S. Hostel Directory and Hitch Hiking Guide when you arrive stateside.

Tom made it here on his cross-country the Saturday that Phil was in the hospital — stayed overnight and left Sun a.m.

He looked very well and seemed to be quite happy and relaxed, although Del Rio is very bad for social life, etc. Mom and I are planning to go to his graduation the end of Oct. if we can "con" you into a "home operation" tour of duty.

All our students are poised for the plunge into school activities — a la Cathy. Your letters indicate you may be going stale as a traveler. Perhaps this is a good sign, and home may look better than it actually is — for a while. Anyway, are anxious for your return.   Love, Dad

These combined letters reached me in Bergen, Norway, where we were staying with relatives of Dale's fiancé, Leif. The mailer with its 11-cent stamp is the only one addressed in Dad's hand, all the others except one from Cathy were in Mom's. I like the coincidence that the last letters were sent to Bergen, Norway, while the very first went to North Bergen, New Jersey.

Dad refers to Dale's brother Wayne, who had offered to meet us in New York. Driving with him back to California would relieve us of planning another 3,000 miles of travel. But, as both parents have by now informed me, that was not going to happen.

Dad mentions my going stale as a traveler and home looking better than it is in response to my comment in a letter from Florence on August 8, "After a tiring day like today — I can begin to count the days. The quiet of home sounds very inviting." On August 16, I commented from Vienna, "Somehow the weather being so gray gets us down, and it would be nice to be home on a day like this instead of in a strange city. Just a mood I guess. But I do miss everyone." My father's assurance that the family was anxious for my return made me happy.

On September 12, two days before receiving these letters in Bergen, I began a letter home. In it I responded to Mom suggesting in hers a month earlier that I look after things while they drove to Tom's graduation from flight school in Texas, which Dad calls a "home operation tour of duty" in this letter.

"I'm really glad I'll be home and able to help make that possible," I say, thrilled that my parents were planning an extended vacation together. I couldn't remember them ever being away for more than a weekend.

In that letter I relate meeting an American military family on the ferry from Germany to Copenhagen, Denmark. Tal and Micki Tweed offered us a ride once we arrived in Copenhagen, where we spent a couple days sightseeing with them and their two children. We experienced the famous Tivoli Gardens together, which was more fun being with kids. Tal is standing behind three intrepid backpackers in the photo in Chapter 2.

I wrote: *By the time we said good-bye we were calling everything ours — our car, our hotel, etc. We all kidded about being part of the family.* Micki wrote me a couple of letters in the succeeding years, including a long one from their duty post in Japan.

While we spent longer and bonded more deeply with the Tweeds than with most people we met, interactions of substance became a hallmark of our travels. These half-century-old documents capture a quest to create connections that went deeper than surface ones travelers usually experience. In my mind, they all are about continually re-creating my family.

We said good-bye to the Tweed family in Copenhagen, and headed for Norway on September 9. Quite miraculously, we met an Irish man packing his van in the hotel lot who offered us a ride to Oslo. We threw in our backpacks and off we went.

After sightseeing in Oslo for two days, Dennis drove us through the mountains all the way to Bergen, on Norway's west coast. He pulled over above a dramatic view of the river to fry chips by the side of the road.

Reading of Phil's illness in Dad's letter led me to check back through the pages of my datebook. I had dreamed of losing Phil nearly a month before, on the night of July 21. Here is how I describe it from a youth hostel near Barcelona, Spain.

> *I woke up during the night – terrible nightmare. Dad had built a trailer for the family like the Hills, except plain. (The Hills used to park a nice motor home on the street by our house, and spend their annual vacation at our pool). And we were all in the back driving these windy roads and the door opened & 4 of the kids fell out & were killed. It was really awful. The only one I knew was Philip – the other three were different from anyone in the family. I couldn't get back to sleep for an hour.*

Mom refers to this dream in her next letter, which describes in more detail the drama of Phil's asthma attack.

Phil being hospitalized the same weekend as Tom's cross-country flight to LA made it seem even more dramatic, and I felt so removed from it all. I was thousands of miles away, busy planning a rendez-vous in London with Fritz, the man I'd met August 15 at St. Stephen's Cathedral in Vienna.

I learned of Phil's hospitalization several days before Dad wrote of it here. Dale's mother mentioned it in the letter to Germany around September 6. She said Dale's brother Wayne, who seems to appear in everyone's letters, and his new fiancée had visited Phil in the hospital.

And in a "Big world/Small world" snippet, I wrote from a U.S. Army post in Germany on August 26 that I'd chatted with a soldier in the post club from Concord, California, where my family had lived from late 1945 until we moved to Berkeley in 1957. He knew a grammar school friend of mine in high school. In an earlier letter home, I'd related meeting someone who knew our next-door neighbor from Concord in the fifties.

Today we'd be calling and texting on cell phones, but in 1966 the planet seemed larger and much less connected than the one we've come to know in the twenty-first century. And yet I had two chance meetings in Europe with people from the small California town where I'd grown up.

CHAPTER TWELVE: YOUR CHILDREN ARE YOUR JEWELS

Letter 18, from Mother: **"I Spent All The Time I Could At The Hospital"**

Postmarked September 8 and received along with the preceding ones from Cathy and Dad in Bergen, Norway, September 12, 1966

Dear Sue,

Haven't heard from you for awhile so didn't know where to write, so I called Cathy's mother & she suggested Bergen – so I'll write there. I got your birthday card & charm & I love both. Dad put my charm on but he put it too close to the other thing I have on it & its kind of lost there, so I'm going to have him move it further on. I show it to everyone. Fritz is quite talented – I hate to admit how stupid I am but I didn't get the full significance of the card until I showed it to Mrs. O'Reilly & she said, "Isn't that nice – the 3 girls with their packs & all the places they visited." I thought it was just 3 tourists. Smart ha? I had a nice birthday. Cathy & Mary took Dad & I out to lunch (Phil came too). It was cute – they paid the bill & all. We went to Bob's. Cathy wanted me to check to see how much Dad would eat – so they'd have enuff money to pay for it. The day before she made a cute invitation that Dad & she & Mary would make dinner. Cathy & Phil made a cake & Dad did the rest. Dad got a pair of gloves for Cathy & Mary to give me & Phil & Jopo gave me a pair of Terry cloth slippers. Phil & I went shopping for it & we had to look in about 4 stores until he got what he wanted.

Tom came home on his cross-country flight & we were so excited – he called on Thurs. nite Aug 18th & said he was sure he'd be coming that weekend. Well, Thurs. nite or early Fri. Morning Phil really got bad (he hasn't been too good part of July and all of Aug). I had to give him two shots. Dad said he almost passed out because of lack of air. Fri. he wasn't bad but I called the Dr. & he put him on cortisone. Fri. evening he started getting bad & the shots weren't helping – so I called the Dr. & we took him to the hospital about 10:30. They thought they'd keep him overnite after a shot of adrenalin. When Dad & I left at midnite he didn't seem so bad & we thought he'd get a good nite sleep in the mist & oxygen tent. When we called about 7 the next morning we found out he had a terrible nite & they were working on him all nite – had to call the Dr. twice. They took his spray away & I guess he must have panicked which doesn't help one's breathing – but I can imagine how horrible it must be to be little in a strange place with strangers & not being able to breathe. I went in about 11 that morning & he was still breathing horribly but they thought he was so much better so he must have been pretty bad. Dr. Siegal was plenty worried & put a special Dr. & a special nurse (he had office hrs) there was a baby with a trachea operation so the special nurse took care of both of them. Phil was in the tent until Mon & had intravenous medication until Mon. afternoon & came home Wed. morning. He got an infection on top of that.

Tom flew into Los Alamitos (near Long Beach) about 2 Sat afternoon. Everyone went to see him fly in except Phil & I. Dad said it was wonderful to see the plane come in especially when its your own flesh & blood flying it. I came home for dinner – had planned to make all Tom's favorites but only got a banana cake made & Dad fixed flank steak. Dave Callahan was at the airport too & stayed & had dinner with us. So we went to the hospital in the evening & then Tom went to see his buddies. He had to be at the airport at 9 in the morning. We hoped to see him take off, (I promised Phil I'd be at the hospital at 11 or near to that time) His flight instructor didn't get there until 10 – so we couldn't see him take off – I was sure sorry. He sure looks good. When I got to the hospital Phil was worse again – they weren't giving him anything for his wheezing but Dr. Siegel came about 1 1/2 hr. later & started the medication over.

I spent all the time I could at the hospital. Phil seems pretty good but he still wheezes quite a bit at times.

Jim was at summer camp during all of this. He was thru Aug 27th & he called the 26th & said Ben Aranda had called him at camp & he was chosen "Alphadelity Man of the Year." They were having the convention in Denver & he flew there to accept his award. He also came in 2nd in the "Athlete of the Camp" out of 180 cadets. He brought a boy home with him – one he met at camp – he was from Georgia Tech

(Savannah Georgia) & he stayed with us for about 3 days. He enjoyed the family.

School has started tho it will really start Mon (half day sessions now). I almost hate to think of the routine starting again. Jerry spent a few days in Concord at the Cavazzas & that Hayborn girl really has him hooked. He talks about going up there & she coming down etc. Remember we thought Jim would be the 1ˢᵗ one married – well right now he's the only one in the running (Jerry).

Cathy has taken over the dishwashing & does a pretty good job of it. Dad still is at home but boy it's wonderful – he's home every nite etc. He's going on a fishing trip with some of the Shell fellows the week of Sept. 19ᵗʰ.

Bought myself some materials to make myself some fall cottons but haven't started any yet. I must get busy. I've put on some weight tho. I guess it's the middle age spread because I don't eat any more than usual.

When Phil was in the hospital & the Dr. was so worried about him I kept thinking of your dream when Phil was killed in that accident. Also a wk. before he went to the hospital he wrote me a note. (We had gone to a ballgame with the Ryans) He said in the note – "I'm wheezing & I took my medicine. In case of death – I leave my material possessions to mother ½, Dad ¼ & Jopo ¼" – so I really thought he had some premonition.

I had a really bad dream about you last nite so I hope you are ok? I can't believe you'll be home by the last of this month.

So long, for now, Love,

Mother

Mom's lengthy letter describes the day after her prior one in Chapter 10, though I received it three full weeks later.

The day after she started that earlier letter on August 18, they rushed Phil to the hospital. Both parents wrote me about the drama that unfolded at the same time I was falling in love in Vienna.

This letter captures the trials of families raising children with health problems. Today childhood asthma is common, and its treatment options extensive. Philip was diagnosed at six months old in 1954 when it was a much rarer condition.

He was five-and-a-half when we moved to LA in 1959. My parents found Dr. Sheldon Siegel, an internationally renowned allergist-immunologist pioneering in asthmatic care for young children in nearby Inglewood. Born and raised in Mom's hometown of Virginia, Minnesota, he was the cousin of Dr. John Siegel, who delivered me at the Virginia Municipal Hospital in 1944.

Dr. Siegel treated Phil into adulthood, at reduced fees. When he died in 2015, Phil sent his siblings a copy of the obituary, which described his contribution to the understanding and treatment of childhood asthma. Mom pretty much credits Dr. Siegel with saving her youngest son's life.

As reported matter-of-factly in this letter, Mother's steady presence at the hospital bed of one sick child kept her from enjoying the triumphs of another. She stoically describes how it all unfolded with only tinges of regret about what she missed.

I love that before my self-deprecating mother describes Phil's illness, she talks in depth about her birthday. I was thrilled she liked my gifts from abroad. She describes being taken out to lunch by Dad and the youngest children, as well as shopping for her present from one of them. She would never have gone to four different stores for herself.

I also love noting that on August 12 of this year, Phil's eldest son was awarded "Active of the Year," an award similar to the one Mom's letter describes Jim receiving in 1966. In 2015 Sam pledged ADG, the same fraternity his uncles Jim, Tom and Gerry, as well as his dad, belonged to at Loyola University.

Mom closes with the dreams she and I had about each other during my travels. They suggest the strength of our energetic connection. Our physical resemblance, which increases as I age, is dramatic.

My mother and I differed dramatically, and we struggled all our lives to surmount the barriers those differences created. When I studied astrology, I learned she was a double Virgo. Her August 31 birthdate may explain some of her great organizing skills and attention to detail, traits which characterize those born under the sign of Virgo. I'm a Gemini, which in astrology is symbolized by the hummingbird, flitting from one place to another. My scattered energy seems to press buttons in all the Virgos I know, including my mother.

My fifty-fifth birthday ("pinchy-pinchy" in the Polish language of her youth), came just twenty days before she died. The "For My Daughter" card she sent, the last written word I received from her, contains this printed message:

You and I

have been through a lot together, yet somehow everything

has always turned out all right. Maybe it's because

we understand each other better than we think we do…

Maybe we're really more alike than we realize…

Whatever the reason,

it means there's a bond between us

that's deeper and stronger than any changes or challenges we've face —

a bond that's not just "parent and child,"

but one that's also heart-to-heart.

Happy Birthday

with Love

She added the note, "I'm mailing your card out early because it will be getting pretty hectic soon. With Love, Mom." It did get very hectic. Loretta Raycraft died unexpectedly around midnight on June 28, 1999.

After suffering severe leg pain for years, she had an angioplasty to unblock a vein in her leg. She told Tom she was pain-free as she came out of surgery, but after lying in the recovery room for a couple hours, it was discovered that the surgery had perforated a vein in her stomach. Her blood type was unavailable, and she died a few hours later on the operating table.

I was in Denver, attending a conference and sharing a hotel room with two friends. Something strange happened when we turned off the lights around midnight. We all witnessed an eerie form of illumination, like a fog of drifting light that seemed to enter through the window and gradually rise to cover the ceiling. I asked my friend in the bed next to me if she saw it.

Here's how Star recalled that shared experience fifteen years later:

> *When we finally turned off the lights we were very aware that something mystical was happening. There was a foggy sort of glowing light in the room that seemed to move around. We even mentioned to each other that it seemed to have some special energy. I remember that we even looked outside to see where the glow could be coming from, and there was no explanation.*
>
> *It seemed to be there for quite some time, and we couldn't figure it out, so I closed my eyes and went to sleep. The next day, after hearing the sad and shocking news, we felt very certain that it was a visitation.*

My experience echoes Star's. It felt like something powerful was happening, and after lying in bed observing the phenomena of drifting, ephemeral light, I closed my eyes and opened my heart. I asked that whatever power was present would bless me and that I might expand to receive all its good.

As I fell asleep, I experienced jewels cascading into the space around me.

It was late the following day when I learned my mother died that night. Hours after receiving the shocking news, I asked my husband what time she had died, and realized it was the same time the drifting light and cascading jewels filled my Denver hotel room.

Mom's close friend, Vanni Mounier, later said she would tell Mom, "Your children are your jewels." I believe those cascading jewels were my mother's way of blessing her children as she surrendered her life.

Vannie also recalls her saying on several occasions, "I have eight kids, and then there's Sue." I interpret those words as my mother's acknowledgment that the help I was able to provide moved me on some level from the category of her child into that of an ally.

Photographs of our growing family often show me holding a baby. I would take the little ones to the park on summer days, and care for them when she cooked elaborate meals with homemade bread. Her visit to that Denver hotel room affirmed our deep and abiding connection. I felt her reaching out to me as the Being of Light into which she was transitioning, unrestricted by physical limits or earthly expectations.

That visitation helped me release guilt about the frustration I may have brought to her last days when the phone system I was marketing caused a glitch in her telephone service. She was unable to receive calls when she returned from her Minnesota trip the day before her death.

Ironically, I'm holding a phone receiver in the last photograph of my mother and me during a 1998 visit to her Redondo Beach home.

The photo was taken by my good friend, Kjerstina, who gave Mom a foot massage to relieve the leg pain she suffered for so long.

Later the family gathered in her home on Calle de Andalucia to share our loss and deal with her things. I woke during the night and wandered through the house, deep in grief and memories. In a cupboard, I found an old container I remembered from childhood, part of a set supermarkets sold at a discount in those days.

On it was a stickie note on which I read, "With Love." I couldn't wait to show my siblings in the morning, thinking Mom had begun labeling things she wanted us to keep, even writing "With Love" on this one. Gerry looked at it and said, "Sue, it says 'Wild Rice'."

Since then, I've closed communications to family members with "Wild Rice," and everyone knows what that means, in their mother's or grandmother's voice.

I believe these letters capture some of my mother's essence. Anchored in her prayerful connection to God through the practice of her Catholic faith, she lived fully and loved all life gave her. I am honored to share the power of her presence in this book, which I feel is my gift to the family she treasured, and the world she made a better place.

In her later years, when she'd see a young mother with her kids, Mom would philosophize that it was more difficult raising even a couple of children now than it had been when she mothered nine. One of her favorite sayings was, "I only remember the good times."

Thanks Mom, I love you.

CHAPTER THIRTEEN: HOMECOMING, LOSS AND LEGACY

Letter 19, from Mother: *"I Know People Are Wondering About The Raycrafts"*

Postmarked Sept 18 and received in London, England Sept 22, 1966

Dear Sue,

Got your card for the Clarks today & your letter the other day. I thought Wally was leaving this weekend so I called her & read the card to her but he's not leaving until Wed. He's staying at Putnam Hall – I think that's what she said. She thought you were just wonderful to remember them. You know Nel – she just raved on & on. I'm mailing the card on to her.

You're freezing & we're roasting – it's 95 or 96 today (you know Sept) & smoggy. So LA ain't too nice right now. Phil has been doing his usual amount of wheezin – the smog doesn't help.

We haven't done any planning for our trip to speak of – I doubt if we'd go to Minn – the weather wouldn't be too hot the end of Oct or 1ˢᵗ of Nov – they could even have snow that early. We're waiting to hear from Tom to kind of determine how we'll plan this trip. If he gets a leave at the time of graduation – I'm sure he'll want to head for home & we would also. Haven't heard from him for 3 weeks. Today (when we called him) he said in that time they had put in their choices of planes they would like to get & would find out in a couple of weeks. I hope to get something next week cause Cathy & I baked something for him & Dad wrote so he'll have to acknowledge those.

I know people are wondering about the Raycrafts – Dad not working & getting a new car in July & now another one. Dad bought a Datsun (Japanese) sedan – maroon. It's a little cheaper than a Volkswagen & he had been reading some good reports on it. It's going to be the boys' car but so far Dad's been driving it around. You know he never gets excited about cars but he surely is about this one. Claims this is the 1ˢᵗ bargain he's ever gotten in a car. We may even drive it to Texas because of the savings in gas. I can't drive a shift but I guess he plans on teaching me.

Don had to fill out a form at school & when he came to the place about where your Father works – he put "unemployed." Father Short called him up after class & asked about it – so Don told him about Shell moving to N.Y. Father said if he needed any help in finding a job let him know - Funny, ha? It may not be so funny next year tho. Don't mention anything about the job. Dad thinks I shouldn't bother you about my dreams etc.

Dad's going fishing next week with some of the Shell fellows.

Jerry has all his classes in the morning so he's driving a laundry truck afternoons. Only started Thurs. & likes it real well but I'm not sure if he'll be able to manage it. Jopo has been working with Don & gets $1.50 an hr. – at least he'll be working for awhile. Phil made the football team at school - which makes him quite happy.

They took pictures of Jim & his trophy at school Thurs so it may be in the local papers. We have the trophy on our mantle & it's about 2-½ ft. high. It's enormous. He gets to keep it this year & then it's passed on

Did you get Dad's letter in Bergen? In case you didn't, Wayne can't come & get you & bring you back because his car won't make it. He tried having it fixed but it needs so much more he's afraid it won't make it across country.

Dear Sue,

I just got back from hoarse back riding it was real fun. I got Sr. Mercedes for a teacher she's alright. Adios

(This little insert is unsigned; I think it's from Cathy as she's the one who spells "hoarse" with an "a.")

Really needs to go back to school – notice the way she spelled "horse" & she forgot the "c" in teacher – which I added.

I have to tell you about the dream I had – I told Mrs. Young & we've been laughing about it. I dreamt you were expecting a baby & it was some boy in Germany. Screwy ha?

Made myself a dress – will start another next week. I wore your pink dress with the lace trim (Easter a couple of years ago) to a Loyola Board meeting & I got a lot of compliments.

Are you going to find time to go to Ireland?

This will be all for now – Phil's been bugging me about going to Steve Kristovisch's. He's still in bed & won't be back in school until Feb.

Best wishes for a safe trip home. Love, Mother

I arrived in Los Angeles just one week after claiming this last of my 19 letters from home. In it Mom shares her fears and thoughts about Dad being unemployed. While later commenting, "Dad thinks I shouldn't bother you about my dreams," she describes her latest one about my being pregnant by a boy in Germany; so interesting in light of my relationship with a German-speaking Austrian.

This letter reached me in London on September 22, where I spent the last days of my European adventure with Fritz, who drove his motorbike across Europe to meet me. My friends and I were ready for our three months saga to be over, and my inviting Fritz to London made its finale more difficult.

When we arrived in New York, we still had a large country to cross. We did that in another "drive-away" car that stalled on a tollway in Pennsylvania, ran down the battery in Indiana, and needed costly repairs in Nebraska. We finally delivered it to Reno, where our boyfriends met us.

The young man I had dated for over a year drove me to Las Vegas where I boarded a plane home. He got to hear that I was in love with another, whom I met on a sidewalk in Vienna; I even showed him pictures. Today I find it hard to believe I was that insensitive.

I returned home from that long summer on Jim's birthday, September 30, 1966. I had nowhere else to go, was physically and emotionally exhausted and grateful to return to the embrace of the family I had grown to appreciate. Robert Frost described my situation perfectly, "Home is the place where, when you have to go there, they have to take you in."

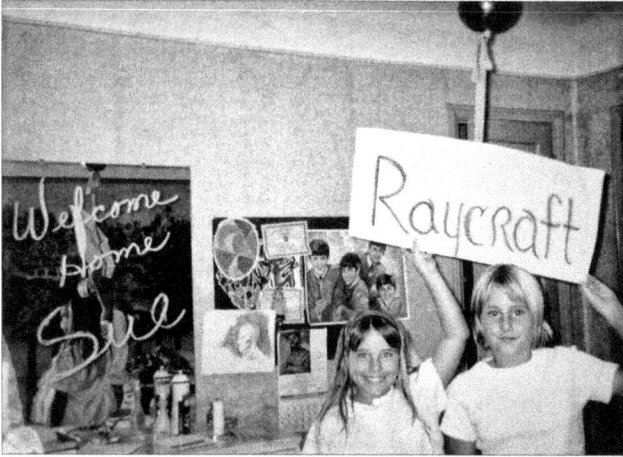

Cathy and Mary welcome me home in the bedroom they happily vacated for their adventuresome older sister.

My first duty was watching kids and tending house for the three weeks my parents traveled to Tom's Flight School graduation in Del Rio, Texas. The 8mm films of their travels through the Southwest, and Mom pinning Tom's wings at the ceremony, still exist.

My next task was to write a term paper required to fulfill my college graduation requirement, as somehow the one I'd turned in for a Sociology of Religion class disappeared. Rushing to leave for Europe, I'd thrown away all the notes and there were no computer back-ups in those days.

I exchanged long letters with my Austrian boyfriend and enjoyed months of rest and recuperation. The words of Harry Belafonte's latest album, "In My Quiet Room," summed up my feelings and I listened to it for hours.

> *Sometimes I sit in the lonely gloom and think how fine it would be*
> *If you could come to my quiet room and share its treasures with me.*

Mom mused in this last letter that people may be wondering about the Raycrafts. Though the primary wage-earner was unemployed they bought new cars and their daughter traveled in Europe for months. When I returned home, no one asked many questions, and daily life went on in the rhythm the letters describe.

Jim's fraternity trophy decorated the living room mantle, everyone who could work had a job, and my young siblings treated me like a conquering hero. I remember feeling grateful for a home where the only pressure I felt was what I put on myself.

I read, worked on my paper and reconnected with friends. I attended several theater performances at Loyola University with Dad. The one I remember was a medieval morality play called *Everyman*.

Like my dream of Phil's accident, and Mom's of me with a German-speaking boyfriend, that play seemed to foreshadow what was to come.

Here's a quote from the introduction to Everyman, written in old English:

Death
I am death that no man dreadeth
For every man I rest, and no man spareth
For it is God's commandment
That all to me should be obedient.

Seven months after my return, around noon on May 2, 1967, in an unexpected and apparently random act of violence, an unknown assailant stabbed Dad to death on a neighbor's lawn. Thus ended the one full year that Mom had promised to wait for his plan to support the family.

The fact that so many choices remained unmade is just one of the many terrible losses of his early death. He had been born on November 3, 1918, and would have turned 48 ½ years old the day after he died.

Though the loss was devastating, the family went on. We seldom spoke of him, keeping our feelings pretty much to ourselves. In fact, one of my poems contains the line, "It's like your family follows an unwritten rule, not to mention your dad or your brother."

I remember cringing at the thought that Dad's murder would become the main thing people thought about us. In July, Dad's killer was arrested in Los Angeles. Lanners Harris was tried and convicted of murder the following year in a heavily reported trial. Sentenced to "Life without the possibility of parole," I discovered during my work on this book that he served just 11 years of that sentence, during a time of leniency in the California prison system.

One of my goals in writing this book is to share my family history unrelated to tragedy and loss. These 19 letters paint a picture of the life my family had lived for a quarter of a century before Dad's death irrevocably changed it.

June 6, 1967 would have been my parents' 25th wedding anniversary. Mom's mother Josephine Wujcik, and sister Marie joined the family at a solemn, tearful Mass in Loyola University's chapel the day after Jim graduated. Neither were the joyous occasions we had all hoped for. In an unexpected twist, Josephine suffered a heart attack and died suddenly when she returned to her Virginia , Minnesota, home; her eldest daughter, Loretta, thus buried her mother and husband within the span of three weeks.

In the months and years that followed, Mom dedicated her considerable energy to raising the children still in her care, supported by Social Security and double indemnity insurance payments for her husband's accidental death.

Shaped by Dad's influence, we committed to honoring what he would have expected of us. Our mutual avoidance of uncomfortable feelings kept family life from changing as much as one might expect.

Since coming to LA, we had used a small tablet hanging by the back door as a "Sign-In sheet." As family members returned from being out at night, each would check off their name. The last one would know to turn out the lights and lock the door.

Soon after the funeral, Don, whose friends from Loyola High came to Dad's Rosary service on the way to their senior prom, looked at the notepad and said, "I guess we won't be needing this anymore." Mom and I both assured him we would need it, that life would go on somehow, though during those first days none of us could imagine how.

My father was unique in many ways. The esteem in which he was held by his family and all who knew him bordered on awe after his sudden death. Ahead of his times in so many ways, I think of him today as a visionary who left us a complex and fascinating legacy.

To illustrate what an extraordinary man Sidney Raycraft was, I compiled the following list of the changing ideas and new possibilities I remember him championing. All have since become mainstream.

Pay TV: There was a measure on the California ballot in 1965 or thereabouts that he strongly supported, believing this innovation was the way of the future, though California voters didn't get it back then.

Anti-smoking campaigns: Dad gathered all his kids in a rare family meeting sometime around 1964, for a serious talk about the dangers of smoking. He observed that as we grew independent we would be tempted by ads and peer pressure to smoke.

He explained that he had smoked for several years, and quit when Mom started because he felt his smoking had influenced her. He also realized by then how dangerous it was. Warning us that the health risks of cigarette smoking had been suppressed, Dad urged all his children to look beyond popular myth to find the truth. In those days the Marlboro Man was still riding off into the sunset, not hooked up to an oxygen machine.

Day-Trading: After he left fulltime employment in mid-1966, Dad made daily visits to the local office of a stock trading company, where he bought and sold commodities and stocks. Ahead of the times in 1966, I didn't hear about small traders doing this until the stock-market booms of the 1980's and 90's. Don shared his recollections of Dad driving to the stock market every day:

> I was a senior and was taking economics 101 in the second semester, early 1967. Dad took me out of school for first-hand experience. We got up early and drove to his "office". He sat me down in front of a big ticker tape machine, gave me a list of stocks to watch for and headed to the commodities market area. He said something about that being where the real money was made. I was the only kid there and was completely bewildered. I took notes and kept jotting down the current value of his stocks. After a while he came back and said he'd done ok. We left and I assumed he was going to take me to lunch and keep me out the whole day, but as I recall, he took me back to school. I guess he realized I needed all the schooling I could get.

Fuel-efficient imports: After driving company cars for years (including a short-lived Edsel in the late 50's) and then buying a variety of his own, ranging from station wagons to a Mustang, Dad found an automobile that excited him. His 1966 Datsun was among the first of the small Japanese cars about to transform the American auto market; Dad immediately bought one and predicted its historical significance.

His was a family that had arrived from Minnesota via Texas by train in 1945, and several years later used their only car as down payment on their first house. In 1966 his mechanic referred to "Mr. Raycraft with his fleet of cars." In those days most families had only one or two autos.

Ronald Reagan: I was either still in college, or had just returned from Europe in 1966 when Dad gave me a copy of a speech by this still largely unknown actor turned politician. He suggested I read it because Reagan, who was elected California governor in 1970, three years after Dad's death, was someone to watch.

Niche marketing: One of Mom's biggest fears was that he would invest in some outlandish idea, like marketing the chili he experimented cooking in the garage. "Raycraft's Own" might have preceded "Newman's Own" by many years. Today, this type of marketing is commonplace.

Talking to babies: I was visiting Mom when Phil arrived with his new baby, Donovan, in 1998. Mom asked why Phil chattered away to a toddler who couldn't understand him. Phil said he remembered Dad doing the same with him as a baby. What father in the fifties knew anything about early childhood development, or took the time to talk to their children as babies?

Finally, the computer revolution: In 1966 and '67 Sid Raycraft was developing a partnership with a man he knew to begin marketing early computer prototypes to colleges. I wish I'd inquired about what he was doing; I don't think any of us did. I can only imagine where the success of those efforts might have led this trail-blazing man who was my father, and the family he loved.

Random hatred and violence, another growing trend that has since become commonplace, denied Dad the opportunity to follow through on any of these plans and dreams. And it began a long learning process for me that culminates in this book.

I close with a poem I wrote in 2008, acknowledging the guidance I have received. I wrote it after Donna LaCour, a high school friend who loved to visit the family in the house on 48th Street, came to see me in Lockwood. She had been my roommate during difficult times, and remains a special friend.

Time wants to show you a different country. It's the one
that your life conceals, the one waiting outside
when curtains are drawn....

From "The Gift" by William Stafford

Donna's Gift: Lifting the Curtain

My father taught me to slice a tomato down, not across;
I'd forgotten that until Donna watched me in the kitchen today,
41 years after violence cut him from our lives.

I'd shared a home with her during my time of forgetting
his huge presence, denying the pain and anger
his murder seeded in me.

She asked; "Why do you slice tomatoes like that?
I learned it from you, and my daughter from me;
but most people don't slice them that way."

Unearthing forgotten memories,
I recall how seriously he took
the small habits of daily living.

Dad observed a tomato sliced top to bottom
holds together better, showing me how that was so:
a foreshadowing in red?

Like waves that never stop lapping the shore,
I feel my father's power, from places deep and hidden,
move me still.

How we slice tomatoes may seem unimportant;
uncovering buried meanings, concealed in small habits,
lifts a curtain on my life.

CHAPTER FOURTEEN: TOGETHER AGAIN

Letter 20, from Jim: *"It Seems That These Days We Have Much To Be Sorry About"*

Undated, postmarked June 14, 1968, in Chandler, Arizona

Dear Sue,

I'm sorry I couldn't write more in my last letter. I was thinking of what a sad wedding anniversary this must have been for Mom and birthday for you, having lost your job. It seems these days there is much to be sorry about – the war, the death of men, the uselessness of what we do (like flying planes to learn to kill more efficiently someone I've never seen and would probably love if he lived next door).

I think I sleep more these days and enjoy it more because I don't have to think or answer for myself when I am asleep.

Have you ever wished maybe you could get out of it all I mean if you had a choice of whether to keep living or being killed? I think I know why the church has so many martyrs-not because they were given a choice between right and wrong; but because they were given a choice of struggling or resting forever.

People weren't made to be saints; it's not natural. I can't write any more. Give my best to Fritz-I like him.

Love, Jim

My brother wrote this letter exactly two years after other family members began theirs to me in Europe in the summer of '66. He mailed it on June 14, 1968, to the family's Los Angeles home where I had lived since my return. Jim mentions the first anniversary of Dad's death (May 2), our parents' 26th wedding anniversary (June 6) and my 24th birthday (June 7), which all took place in the weeks before his letter.

Jim died on November 12, 1971, 3 ½ years after he wrote about being "given a choice of struggling or resting forever." The C-130 he was training Vietnam-bound pilots to fly crashed in Little Rock, Arkansas, killing all but one of its crew. Jim's death 4 ½ years after Dad's opened wounds that had finally begun to heal.

Always proud of his Texas roots, Jim was born September 30, 1945, in Amarillo, near the wartime facility in Cactus, Texas, where Dad worked as a chemical engineer. The family had moved there from Mother's parents' in Virginia, Minnesota, where I'd been born the day before D-Day in 1944. He was my parents' third child in as many years, and perhaps their most sensitive. After chiding him for being chubby during our college years, I found him wiping away tears in front of the bathroom mirror.

James, Susan and Thomas Raycraft (from the left) in first professional photograph, 1947.

When I discovered this letter to his sister nearly fifteen years later, Jim became my guide to the deep inner work this chapter records, as I detail below. I wrote in my journal a week after receiving it that I saw "different ways I could direct the energy of my life." It took nearly two more decades to begin releasing the anger and pain losing my father and brother generated, which had become substantial barriers to that self-direction.

Denying those uncomfortable feelings created emotional and psychological problems that I struggled for years to understand and heal. Finishing this book is another step in that process, freeing me once again, on an ever deepening level.

The years following those two deaths were chaotic ones in my life. When I received this letter, I had just postponed my June wedding to Fritz and then been laid off from my first post-college job. Less than a month later, I accepted a job teaching Head Start in Oakland and moved to Berkeley.

I stayed there just five months, and in early 1969 returned to Los Angeles. After ending my relationship with Fritz, I immediately got involved with a man as different from me in age and experience as I could find, which continued off and on for three years, through early 1972.

And right in the middle of this time of great change, after summer trips to New York in 1969 and 1970, I moved to New York City for eight months (Aug '70–March '71). My journal, which I began in 1968 and continue today, records a very conflicted person struggling to know herself while desperately running from that self, always reacting to others.

That Christmas I spent hours shopping in Macy's and other NYC stores for gifts to send each family member. It was the only time in my entire life I veered from our custom of only giving to the one whose name you'd drawn.

My interest in writing surfaced in early 1971 in NYC, and I took a class nurturing it at New York University. Returning to LA that May, I became "Community Participation Coordinator" in the suburb of Cerritos, a job my boss and friend Federico Grabiel and I molded around my natural talents. Publishing a newsletter stimulated me to write more, and I began dabbling in poetry.

I quit that job and left the Los Angeles area for Lake Tahoe in 1973. There I met my future husband, Larry Woodfill, and we moved to Visalia. I worked with him building houses for a couple of years and then designed a federally funded pilot project training women in non-traditional jobs, based on the experience.

Part of the "back-to-the-land" movement of the 1970s, Larry and

I bought 40 acres of pristine rolling hills in 1977 in a place called Lockwood, in the San Antonio Valley of California's central coast. I later discovered it is thought to be named for the first woman to run for U.S. President, in 1884 and 1888. I wrote and produced a play about Belva Lockwood for the post office centennial in 1986.

After sharing the joys and frustrations of living without modern conveniences for a while, in 1979 I took a state job in King City, the closest small town. I was still mostly running from myself.

In 1982 I joined Al-Anon, seeking tools to shift my focus from problems belonging to others. Al-Anon prepared me for the healing I so desperately needed. I learned to let go of the compulsion to change those around me, and begin caring for myself. The first of the Twelve Steps of Al-Anon, adopted from AA, "I admitted I was powerless, that my life had become unmanageable," became pivotal for me.

At about this time I discovered a lump expanding beneath my left ear. A doctor from Stanford recommended its immediate removal. He told me it was growing into the nerve that controlled the facial muscles used to talk, smile and frown. While warning me of the tumor's effects, he could say nothing as to what might have caused it. After it was surgically removed and found to be benign, I looked for clues as to its origin in my diet and other life choices.

I read a lot of Shirley MacLaine in those days. She theorized that all ailments begin on subtle energetic realms, slowly growing more tangible until entering the densest plane, the physical, where they finally get our attention. Dr. Good told me the tumor on my parotid gland could grow into the nerves that control my facial muscles and impact my physical ability to express feelings. Considering that since my father's death had upended my 22-year-old world, I'd ignored, avoided, and denied so many of mine, had my wounded spirit finally said "enough" and begun sending a message to my body?

It took me a few more years to respond to the wake-up call sounded by the many levels of pain I was experiencing. Rolfing, therapy, and writing moved me toward acknowledging that I needed to change.

I gathered my journals, wrote more poetry, and asked the Universe for help. Jim came to me in Dreamtime and directed me to this letter. I dreamt he had left a message in a journal that would provide me a key. The next morning, I found this letter in a pile of materials stacked on the floor by my bed. Reading it as though for the first time, something shifted and opened within me.

It was as though my brother reached across time and through the veil between life and death to shatter the dam of denial I had been living behind for 17 years. Reading Jim's thoughts helped me consider that we do, on mysterious and subtle levels I may never fully understand, participate in choosing our path to death. That profound message, delivered in such a dramatic way, prepared me to release him and Dad.

The next step in the process soon appeared. I asked my new friend, Alice Larsen, a Catholic nun who worked at a nearby correctional facility, for advice. I thought that because she worked in prisons, she might connect me with the person who had killed Dad, and that would help me face my buried feelings.

Alice told me I needed to start with myself, to uncover my feelings and begin to accept and process them. She helped me understand that my problems were not about anyone else. She recommended a practitioner of a technique from Scientology called "Auditing," and explained how this precise method had helped her deal with repressed emotions.

Since I didn't have a clue how or where to start healing myself, I followed my friend's suggestion. Using the analogy of a tape recorder storing one's feelings about all their experiences, the practitioner began the process of defusing the power buried in my memories. I followed his instructions, sitting in a dark room listening to categories of feelings and tearfully speaking mine, over and over.

This technique is something a therapist might have shared, had my friend recommended a different route. I did nothing further through Scientology, which I am reluctant to endorse due to concerns many have expressed. I describe it to illustrate that when I became willing to change, help appeared.

Once I took this first step, one I would never have thought of on my own, only barely understood, and did rather blindly, my life began to shift. Everywhere I turned a path toward healing seemed to appear.

I began seriously writing poetry. I wrote poems about others, and what I thought they needed. I realize rereading them today that I was speaking to myself. I could see more clearly in others the issues I faced, like putting their needs above my own.

Another valuable step on my healing journey began in April 1985. I organized Women's Healing Weekends at Sun Mountain, a research center founded by friends George and Maia Ballis in the Sierra foothills above Fresno. I became a member of their Board of Directors, and for the next three decades Sun Mt. grounded my healing journey.

During one of my early visits to Sun Mountain's library, filled with books on every sort of health-giving system, I asked my Higher Power to show me what I needed. I picked up Dr. Edward Bach's *Heal Thyself*, and as I read its first words, I knew the author held another key to my healing path. Dr. Bach introduced Flower Essences to the world in the 1930s.

Like Shirley MacLaine, he believes physical disease is the gross manifestation of what begins on the subtle planes of our consciousness. Disharmony between our soul, our divine nature and our personality/mind creates disease in the body. It can also grow from cruelty or wrongs done to us by others, which Bach describes as sins against Unity. The purpose of disease is to bring the personality back to the Divine Will of the Soul. The pain and suffering of illness help teach us lessons we have failed to grasp.

Dr. Bach's words made absolute sense to me. I had avoided untangling and processing my feelings; the resulting disharmony eventually became dense enough to manifest on the physical level as a tumor threatening the nerve that controlled my expression of feelings. I could see the effects of the disharmony in all aspects of my life, from relationships to career to self-worth.

My soul knew my father and brother were following their unique life paths, but my personality didn't want to release them. By choosing to hold tight to the limiting belief that I had lost them through death, I was committing a sin against the Unity of All Life; I was now learning to let go and to forgive myself.

At Sun Mountain I studied the Bach Flower Essences with Maia, which I continue to use and share. Her husband and Sun Mountain co-director Elfie introduced me to Shamanic drumming, another powerful tool for change. I will never forget my participation in Sun Mountain's first Drumming Circle at the close of 1985.

About 20 of us crammed into the basement, dubbed "The Womb." To the steady rhythm of many drums, we began individual and collective journeys. I felt I was being blown open, and escaped into the outside air with a pounding headache. I returned to the womb and continued drumming.

Connecting with a group dedicated to personal honesty and inner growth guided by sacred practices was life changing for me. I regularly drove four hours to Sun Mountain for long weekends with my drumming circle. We came together as a tribe, to explore the themes and issues that limited us, and the beliefs we were ready to release, always guided by the drums echoing the steady heartbeat of Mother Earth.

Gathering scattered selves, we invented ritual and created community. We made masks, held each other in our collective lap and journeyed together into sacred space. Elfie's chants summoned the kid elves of Sun Mountain to pray and play with us as we dreamt and drummed ourselves whole. I wrote poems. Maia painted powerful Shamanic visions and has continued contributing to my healing process by designing the cover of this book.

Other ceremony called me to reconnect with some of the influences of my upbringing. Praying the Rosary and attending weekly, and sometimes daily Mass with my family were powerful childhood experiences. I had lost any connection to the spirituality they represented.

On the first weekend of May 1985, Alice and I gathered with a group called "Woman-Church West" at the Catholic girls' high school I had attended my freshman year in Berkeley. Again, through ceremony, I faced my personal experience of how the institutional church had failed to embody Christ's message of equality. That Sunday, women celebrated the Eucharist blessed by female hands, helping me release the sting of exclusion felt by many girls who grow up Catholic. My poem about that experience captures its effect on me at the time.

Unspoken not silent, forgotten not finished
Broken not severed, umbilical chord, church of my mother

Repressed not released, shunned not forgiven
Buried not dead, funeral dirge, church of my father

Compassion not catechism, commitment not confession
Truth, peace and justice, church of my own

In 1986 I responded to recurring family problems by moving away
for a time. After working seven years in the King City office of the
Employment Development Dept., I transferred to Watsonville. On
one of my first days at the job, I met a woman who gave me my new
name, "SuRay," which I gradually began using. Michelle Shippen
looked at me and stated with absolute clarity, "Susan Raycraft, I'm
going to call you SuRay, because you are a ray of sunshine in this
place."

After years doing job training and development, I was ready for a career change. Selected to teach new employees, I began to travel and
teach throughout Central California. In Santa Cruz, I made friends
among New Age circles and learned to meditate as I became involved in a global gathering for peace on December 31, 1986. Drawn
to people modeling new ways of being in the world, my attachment
to old thought patterns no longer serving my highest good lessened.
I gradually grew into the dynamic woman I describe in my poem,
Direction, in Chapter 6.

I returned home, and back to work in the Salinas Valley in 1990. A
few years later I was able to share the deep inner work I had done
around the issues of death and loss with my friend Dalene Modena
as she confronted cancer. I would write her long letters, and our profound discussions about her approaching transition birthed the idea
of this book. I still treasure Dalene's note from that time, "With gratitude and love for the nurturing and grounding and heartfelt love
and support."

I close the record of a decade of personal healing with the poem I
wrote about the effect of Jim's pivotal letter, which began that journey in 1985. Like Mom's comments about pea soup in one of her later
letters, Jim's words spoke a nearly complete poem.

To Jim: Resting Forever

Growing up with six brothers
I learned caring for others;
To love baseball and bicycles,
And take charge in a crowd.

One brother left us, not long after Dad did
Filling me up with anger and pain;
Feelings which took as much energy to keep in,
As they pushed with to get out.

> *In the mountains a seer told me:*
> *To face death without fear, let go you and Dad*
> *Only then can my own needs, my inestimable value,*
> *Fill up the emptiness you left behind.*

> *She said you are still with me,*
> *In another dimension, which is all around us*
> *That my holding on denies you the freedom*
> *You have attained.*

In a dream you told me you'd left me your journal
Which led to the letter I'd kept by my bedside.
I reread the words a young pilot wrote to his sister
Not long before dying.

"These days we have much to be sorry about,
The war, the death of men, the uselessness of what we do,
(Like flying planes to learn to kill more efficiently someone
I've never seen and would probably love if he lived next door)."

> *"Have you ever wished maybe you could get out of it all?*
> *I mean if you had a choice of whether to keep living*
> *Or being killed?*
> *A choice of struggling or resting forever."*

> *"People weren't meant to be saints; it's not natural."*
> *And you ended the letter, "I can't write anymore."*
> *Jim, we each make our own choices,*
> *In death, as in life.*

Learning this truth from you frees me
To feel pain and anger, hear my own voices
Telling me I have to release you
From holding back feelings I need to let go.

This awareness empowers me
To learn life's hardest lessons
And speak them out loudly
Knowing thus we will be together again.

Jim was the first of the nine siblings to marry. I clearly recall asking him how he found the courage to make such a commitment. He laughed and assured me he didn't feel courageous, that he was just doing what felt right to him. His message that we're not called to be saints, but to live our truth continues to inspire me.

Wearing the shiny gold dress my mother made for the occasion, Jim and I dance at his wedding to Gail Philen on October 4, 1969. He may be wondering, "Who me, brave?" in response to my question, above.

When he died a brief three years later on November 10, 1971, Jim's daughter Kelli had just turned a year old. She spent a lot of time around the Raycraft family growing up, and as her eldest granddaughter, was especially close to her Grandmother Loretta.

At a family gathering someone mentioned that Kelli never knew her father, and she looked around the circle of aunts and uncles and replied, "Oh I knew my dad, I knew him through all of you." On New Year's Day 2017, I officiated at Kelli's wedding to her new husband, Mitch. I invited Jim's spirit to bless his daughter and her newly blending family. Jim's clear presence blessed us all.

After performing the ceremony uniting the Manos and Flanagan families, Aunt Su stands with the Flanmanosagans, the blended name Mitch and Kelli enjoy calling themselves now. Jake (front middle), Christopher, and Emily are Jim's grandkids. Mitch's son Travis is next to Emily in the back row.

On November 7, 2013, Loyola-Marymount University dedicated a memorial to alumni who died serving their country. A reporter photographed me touching my brother's name engraved in black marble, and the picture appeared on the Los Angeles Loyolan on Veteran's Day of that year.

CHAPTER FIFTEEN: PERSONAL AND PLANETARY

The story this book records has accompanied me for half a century, helping create the canvas on which I've painted my life. I publish it the year of the fiftieth anniversary of my father's death, an event that altered my reality and directly affected my development.

In the prior chapter, I detail the life lessons I have learned from the loss of my father and my brother. That completing the book has taken me a full half-century signifies how we humans hang on to our pain, and that becoming whole is the process of a lifetime.

I conclude my story with a perspective beyond healing from personal loss. In this final chapter, I seek to connect my experience and those lessons with the experience of others and the wider world.

Healing is both personal and planetary, individual and communal. My intention is to give my story to the planet, to transmute its individuality into universality by closing with the bigger picture.

I know my father's death took place and has been viewed within that wider context. I recently overheard a cousin whom I had last seen at Dad's funeral in 1967 saying, "He was murdered by a black man for no reason," reminding me of that fact. Two possibilities have concerned me over the years; first, that Dad's murder might become the main thing people thought about his family, and secondly, that it would be used to justify hatred and bigotry.

The period on which this memoir focuses was a time of intense social and political change. I began the journals I still keep on March 2, 1968, and on April 4, I wrote, "Today was a tragic one for our nation . . . Martin Luther King was shot to death. And we heard today that the man who killed Dad was found guilty."

In June of that same year, following Robert Kennedy's assassination, an editorial I still have appeared in the neighborhood newspaper, which we also still had in those days. Its author compared King's and Kennedy's deaths to my father's, along with an LA policeman killed while on duty.

The deaths of two famous and two unknown men, including Sidney T. Raycraft, named three times in the piece, were blamed on "the failure of our legislative and judicial branches of government to properly control the sale of firearms and to justly punish criminals."

The editor goes on to endorse the death penalty and decry "the breakdown in respect for fellow man and for law and order which is sweeping this nation." The solution: to "begin following clean-cut leaders who speak with clear heads rather than those who speak from platforms with minds fogged by hate and drugs." He closes by blaming individuals rather than society, which "did not wield the knife that slashed the life away from Sidney Raycraft."

I quote that editorial to indicate how little has changed in our nation's struggle to understand the causes and cures for crime.

In October of 2016, during my work on this book, the Oakland Museum observed the fiftieth anniversary of the founding of the Black Panthers in Oakland, California, seven months before Dad's death. I visited the exhibit, which deeply moved me.

I learned Bobby Seale and Huey Newton, students at Merritt Community College in Oakland, founded the Black Panther Party for Self-Defense on October 22, 1966. It was three weeks after I returned from my European adventure. Inspired by Dr. Martin Luther King's Oakland speech of December 28, 1962, the year I graduated from high school, party leaders drafted a platform calling for full employment for black people, decent housing, the release of blacks from jails and prisons, and an end to police brutality.

Sound familiar?

Six months later, on May 2, 1967, the same day my father was stabbed multiple times near his Los Angeles home by a stranger who was black, Seale led a group of Panthers carrying arms into the state Capitol in Sacramento. They were protesting a law restricting the right to bear arms, passed in response to the Panthers' armed patrols of their neighborhoods. In another interesting twist of history, the National Rifle Association supported that law. Today the NRA fights against any control of guns by any arm of government for any reason.

The very existence of the Black Panther Party and its mobilizing effects on ordinary African-Americans challenged the country's white majority. The FBI and local law enforcement targeted everything the Panthers did anywhere, focusing on the fact that a few members committed violent acts, a small part of the larger truth. Mostly the Panthers worked for community programs to raise the economic and safety levels of seriously dispossessed people. Such programs spread into ghettos across the country and around the world.

The Oakland Museum exhibit documented, from the historical vantage point of five decades, how this relatively small group of black women and men spoke truth to a society that could deny that truth by destroying those speaking it.

Many died; some remain imprisoned today. They provoked more violence than they practiced. Acknowledging that the American Black Panther Party spoke truth to a culture in denial is a step toward healing. The larger Civil Rights movement, of which the Panthers were a radical arm, challenged that same denial throughout the country.

Progress toward equal treatment lying at the heart of the American Civil Rights movement continues today with groups like Black Lives Matter. And the reality that inequality in law and institutions still exists becomes harder to deny when cellphone videos capture it.

As this book goes to press, we are observing the 50th anniversaries of events in Detroit and Chicago similar to the Watts riots of 1965, to which my father refers in his first letter; he actually used the word "rumbles." Today they are usually called "rebellions" rather than "riots," as all such disturbances have been known since before the Civil War, in the troubled racial history of the United States.

My using the word "riot" in reference to Dad's comment in Chapter 2 was appropriate. Today I too name them rebellions.

And my father was a victim of what is called racism, as much as were Huey Newton, Bobby Seale, and Martin Luther King, Jr. History records that fear and hatred of the "other" have torn apart communities, cultures, and families throughout time.

I intend this book contributes to bringing us together.

101

In his 2015 book, *Between the World and Me,* Ta-Nehisi Coates challenges our understanding of the term "racism" by which we explain all manner of societal ills, as he ponders how to prepare his black son to grow up in America.

> *I saw that what divided me from the world was not anything intrinsic to us but the actual injury done by people intent on naming us, intent on believing that what they have named us matters more than anything we could ever actually do. In America, the injury is not in being born with darker skin with fuller lips, with a broader nose, but in everything that happens after.*

And while my father's murder may have been what we now call a "hate crime," Coates's paradigm helps explain why I chose to move beyond viewing it primarily as that. I did not want my experience to be used to define a single group of people on any level.

On the day of my father's funeral, I stood with several of his close friends around a barbecue pit near the garage. One of them mentioned the murder in angry, racially-charged terms. I recall throwing something I held into the pit's fire, vowing to release from my life the energy those words represented.

I would refuse to join the circle of pain and recrimination Dad's racially motivated killing could fuel. I would not allow what a stranger did to my father on the streets of Los Angeles to define those belonging to the same race. Nor would I let it determine the feelings I carried into my future.

When I returned to my job with a Compton Head Start program, a colleague tearfully shared her dream with me. She saw my father and told him how guilty she felt that one of her people had done this. He replied, "Don't worry, Sue will understand." Crying with her, I prayed for such understanding.

In our last year together, my father gifted me a beautifully bound copy of Teilhard de Chardin's *Building the Earth.* Chardin challenges us to reach a higher plane of humanity through death and rebirth. In his vision, the experience of great loss allows us to become part of the spirit of the Earth.

All that lives will die. For some people, like Sidney Raycraft, death seems to come "before their time," or in ways that appear senseless.

Teilhard's vision of such deaths as dying to self and transmuting into the spirit of Earth has helped me heal. I have come to believe in the decades since Dad's dramatic death that my father was called to die to self that we who live might be transformed.

While avoiding judgments based on race has remained a constant in my life, failing to acknowledge the anger and pain I felt at losing my beloved father created personal problems that took me years to uncover and process. Finishing this book is another way for me to transmute personal loss.

"Don't write about SOMETHING," Bob Dylan says, "Write about EVERYTHING." The SOMETHING of which I write is the simple life and profound love of one family glimpsed through the lens of twenty letters written in the span of two years. The story is as particular, as unique as a couple of years in anyone's life can be.

The EVERYTHING? The call to understand and communicate that leads me to share my experience and what it has taught me. The story shared through the letters does not close with my father's violent death. It closes with the healing of self and others, which is truly the journey of a lifetime.

In June 2016, thanks to the Episcopal Diocese of El Camino Real, I experienced Healing of Memories, which brings together victims and perpetrators of violence in small group, face-to-face interactions. Fr. Michael Lapsley, a priest who lost both hands and much of his hearing in a 1990 letter-bombing during South Africa's struggle to end apartheid, created the program in 1998.

Michael has taught HOM around the world, particularly in places where people have been gravely wounded, like Rwanda and Northern Ireland. Its intimate format allows participants to unwind and release painful aspects of their lives by sharing their stories.

Everyone has suffered. We have all been imprinted energetically by things done to us, and things we have done to others that caused pain. My story is a perfect example, and the fact that it happened half a century ago reminds us how profoundly loss impacts every level of one's being across time.

When one person heals, the whole community benefits. We all learn from each one's deeper understanding of how and why violence happens.

A German woman who directs a concentration camp memorial is quoted by Father Lapsley in his book, *Redeeming the Past: My Journey from Freedom Fighter to Healer.*

> [L]iberation from a lifelong struggle with shame and guilt [comes] not in suppressing, but in remembering; not in justification, but admission; not in weighing one against the other, but in the willingness to mourn and be sorry; not in bitter retreat into protective arguments, but in asking for forgiveness.

In Fr. Lapsley's words:

> Healing work . . . requires quiet focused attention, and it rewards us with the satisfaction that comes from witnessing the transformation of pain and sometimes bitterness into a measure of peace and hope.

Honoring and sharing my path from suppression to remembering, and from there to mourning, forgiving and sharing brings me great joy. I release the past to which I have remained bound. I live today to its fullest. Fifty years feels like a long time for this to take. And it is all perfect.

I closed Chapter 13's tribute to my father with a poem quoting "The Gift" by William Stafford:

> Time wants to show you a different country. It's the one
> that your life conceals, the one waiting outside
> when curtains are drawn....

I am grateful to Time for gently teaching me to draw the curtains and reach INSIDE. Everything I need is right here.

I thank the parents who taught me to love and the family with whom I learned to share love.

This is the country we inhabit, the one we create today.

www.ingramcontent.com/pod-product-compliance
Lightning Source LLC
Chambersburg PA
CBHW050014090426
42734CB00020B/3263